How to use this workbook

Structure

The activities in this workbook will help you to develop the skills and knowledge that you will need to achieve your best grade in AS/A-level English Literature, whichever exam board specification you are following.

Each section offers a clear structure with activities that gradually increase in difficulty:

- **Starting out:** accessible activities that offer an introduction to the topic.
- **Developing your ideas:** skills-building activities that look in more detail at particular aspects of the text.
- **Taking it further:** more challenging tasks that will test your understanding of the text and consolidate your learning.

Boosting your skills

The final chapter of the workbook offers exam-focused activities that allow you to apply the skills you have developed. It also includes step-by-step guidance on the Assessment Objectives, and how to cover them in your written responses.

Features

Key terms

Definitions of key concepts and terminology. Understanding these and using them correctly in your written responses will help you to gain marks for AO1.

Key skills

Concise explanations of important skills to develop during your AS/A-level studies. A variety of skills are covered – from fundamental ones such as analysing the structure of a text or embedding quotations in your writing, up to more advanced skills that are necessary to gain the top grades, such as exploring different interpretations of characters.

Challenge yourself

Advanced tasks that will push you further and help prepare you to achieve your best grade in the exams. They often focus on context (AO3), connections between texts (AO4) or critical interpretations of them (AO5).

Answers can be found at: **www.hoddereducation.co.uk/workbookanswers**

Introduction

Since its first performance in 1613 or 1614, *The Tragedy of the Duchess of Malfi* has always been an energetic and thought-provoking play that varies in each production. Webster was a true Renaissance thinker, questioning whether people should be promoted on merit rather than social standing, whether ecclesiastical officials should wield so much worldly power, and whether it would be possible for a ruler to abolish corruption from his or her court and appoint only wise counsellors. He chooses as his main protagonist a strong and independent woman, raising the questions of whether women really should be totally controlled by men, whether it is possible to reconcile duty with personal happiness, and what is the nature of true love. He directly addresses new and revolutionary theories; for instance, he treats madness as a psychological illness rather than demonic possession.

To bring these issues to the stage, Webster exploits all of the styles and dramatic forms he had inherited. He makes much use of darkness, newly made possible with indoor theatres, as well as incorporating a ghostly echo, a subversion of a court masque, a dumb show, disguises, etc., employing them to help him to explore his themes and the psychology of his characters. It is very important to remember that what you have been given to study is not a novel but a play, so do make sure you watch at least one production, either in the theatre and/or on film.

Studying *The Tragedy of the Duchess of Malfi* at AS/A-level and using this workbook

Your study of Shakespeare for Key Stage 3 and GCSE will form a good basis as you approach *The Duchess of Malfi* for AS/A-level. However, you will now need to develop your existing skills alongside a more detailed understanding of the text. Activities in this workbook have been designed to support you in this process.

In particular, you will need to be more aware of different critical approaches, which is why this workbook devotes Chapter 6 to them. Throughout the workbook, you will also encounter perspectives from a range of critics and other readers to help you to develop your own response to the play. You will also need to consider the historical, literary and biographical contexts of *The Duchess of Malfi*, and so Chapter 5 in this workbook focuses in detail on how these aspects have influenced the play.

You still need to study characterisation at A-level, but you will be expected to have a deeper awareness of characters' dramatic roles, and the dynamics between them, carefully avoiding the trap of writing about them as if they are real people. Chapter 3 covers Characterisation, and the exercises will help you to develop a critical approach when you watch a production of the play.

Themes remain important, but you will need to show more awareness of how Webster's themes are reflected in the language of the play, and to be able to demonstrate how Webster has employed his skills as a playwright to develop his key ideas and concerns. Exercises in Chapter 2 will help you to form your own opinions of Webster's key themes and how he has explored them in the play.

An important skill for students of literature is the ability to analyse the ways that meanings are shaped. Activities in both Chapter 4 (Form, staging and language) and Chapter 1 (Plot and dramatic structure) will draw further attention to how Webster has crafted *The Duchess of Malfi*, and the subtle ways in which he weaves together dramatic devices, structure, plot, form and language into a cohesive whole.

You need to develop your own interpretation of the play and be able to express this confidently, supporting your argument with evidence from the text. You should be able to remember the Act, and ideally the scene, in which any major event or speech occurs, so that you can find them easily. An overview of the play will help you to analyse the play's narrative arc and to relate this to the genre of tragedy.

You do not necessarily have to attempt all the activities in the workbook — you could select according to your needs. However, there is a progression within each section, from the basics in 'Starting out' to the more challenging 'Taking it further' activities. In addition, 'Challenge yourself' boxes aim to help you achieve the top grades. You should also take note of the 'Key terms' and 'Key skills' boxes to widen your critical vocabulary, and to help you write the fluent, well-structured, sophisticated essays that will bring success at this advanced level.

Act, scene and line references are to the fifth New Mermaids edition, published by Bloomsbury Methuen and edited by Brian Gibbons. These will vary slightly in other editions, but the short quotations will help you to overcome these variations.

Answers can be found at: www.hoddereducation.co.uk/workbookanswers

Plot and dramatic structure

Early modern playwrights were more concerned with the dramatic significance of events than with creating a detailed time frame for them. Although we can calculate that the action of *The Duchess of Malfi* takes place over several years, the only indication of how many is the age of Antonio's son at the end of the play when Delio describes him as 'a pretty gentleman', indicating that he is probably at least 6 or 7 years old. We know from his horoscope that he was born in 1504, so presumably Antonio and the Duchess married in 1503, if not before. It is important to recognise that the action of the play takes place over a lengthy time span, allowing for the growth and development of the main characters as the pressure under which Webster puts them takes its toll.

Plot

STARTING OUT

1   On a separate piece of paper, summarise events in the play.
2   How well do you know the play? Circle the correct answer in the statements below.
   (a) At the beginning of the play, Antonio has just returned from:
      A   England
      B   Denmark
      C   France.
   (b) Bosola is given the position of:
      A   Master of the Duchess' household
      B   Provisor of the Duchess' horse
      C   Master of the Duchess' estates.
   (c) Antonio, the Duchess and their children pretend to go on a pilgrimage to:
      A   the shrine of Our Lady of Loretto
      B   the shrine of Our Lady of Mentorella
      C   the shrine of Our Lady of Pompeii.
   (d) The Cardinal is stabbed by:
      A   Bosola
      B   Antonio
      C   Ferdinand.

DEVELOPING YOUR IDEAS

Webster's source

3   Webster based his play on a real-life event, using as his main source *The Palace of Pleasure* by William Painter (1566–1567). However, Webster's play has a number of significant differences from his source. In the right-hand column of this chart, explain what you think Webster has gained or lost from these alterations. One has been done for you.

THE PALACE OF PLEASURE	THE DUCHESS OF MALFI
A Neither of the brothers warns the Duchess against remarriage.	The juxtaposition of their threatening warnings and the clandestine marriage makes the audience aware, from the start of the play, of the danger the lovers are facing. This is emphasised by the Duchess' soliloquy [1.1.331–339].

CONTINUED ➔

THE PALACE OF PLEASURE	THE DUCHESS OF MALFI
B The Duchess tells Antonio to flee because 'If you do tarry, you will be the cause of the ruin and overthrow of us all'.	
C Antonio is reluctant to leave; he does not care about his own death, but he believes that the Duchess will be in danger if he stays.	
D The Cardinal does not have a mistress.	
E The Duchess does not pretend to accuse Antonio of cheating her.	
F There is no account of tortures inflicted on the Duchess.	
G Delio is a stranger who only comes into the story at the end to warn Antonio that the Duchess and her children have been murdered and his own life is in danger.	
H Ferdinand does not go mad.	
I The Cardinal and Ferdinand are not killed.	
J Bosola only comes in at the end. He is hired to kill Antonio, then escapes.	

Challenge yourself

Borrowing a plot

TS Eliot wrote about the fact that writers borrow material from others, pointing out that:

The good poet welds his theft into a whole of feeling which is unique, utterly different than that from which it is torn; the bad poet throws it into something which has no cohesion.

Eliot TS (2000), *Philip Massinger, The Sacred Wood*, New York, www.Bartleby.com.

Answers can be found at: www.hoddereducation.co.uk/workbookanswers

Bearing in mind that Webster has used an existing story and altered it to suit his purposes, consider what TS Eliot is saying here. How far do you agree that Webster is a good poet/dramatist who has used his source to create something utterly different?

KEY SKILLS

Including textual details

Although you should avoid re-telling the story, you should try to include textual details from the play to show you have a thorough understanding: 'To convey her absolute loyalty, Cariola promises to 'conceal the secret from the world', with the same care that poisoners keep the poison from their children, a simile which emphasises the extreme danger the lovers are in.'

Hidden listeners

4   Several times, Webster has characters hidden who overhear speeches without the speaker's knowledge. In each of the following examples, explain how these dramatic devices advance the plot.

(a) In Act 1 scene 1, Cariola overhears the Duchess wooing Antonio.

....

....

....

(b) In Act 3 scene 2 lines 60–67, Ferdinand overhears the Duchess talking about Antonio.

....

....

....

(c) In Act 5 scene 2 lines 216–271, Bosola overhears the Cardinal murder Julia.

....

....

....

(d) In Act 5 scene 4 lines 29–31, Bosola hears the Cardinal plan his death.

....

....

....

War

5 The story unfolds against a background of military activity; even the Cardinal is asked by the Holy Roman Emperor to lay aside his robes and take up arms. Clearly, he was a successful military commander before he took his vows. Locate the other references which suggest that war may be imminent:

QUOTATION		SOURCE
A	FERDINAND: When shall we leave this sportive action and fall to action indeed?	1.1.88–89
B	FERDINAND: Good Lord Silvio, / Do us commend to all our noble friends / At the leaguer.	
C	MALATESTE: [*Shows plan*] Here's a plot drawn for a new fortification, / At Naples.	
D	DELIO: A marginal note in the muster-book that he is / A voluntary lord.	
E	FERDINAND: Draw me out an hundred and fifty of our horse, / And meet me at the fort bridge.	
F	DIVERS CHURCHMEN: Lead bravely thy forces on, under war's warlike banner:	
G	CARIOLA: Look, madam, what a troop of armed men / Make toward us.	
H	JULIA: You shall not need follow the wars, / I'll be your maintenance.	
I	DELIO: This fortification / Grew from the ruins of an ancient abbey.	
J	DELIO: Let us make noble use / Of this great ruin; and join all our force / To establish this young hopeful gentleman / In's mother's right.	

6 Webster never makes it clear who the enemy may be, and there is no fighting during the play, so why do you think Webster chose to have preparations for war being made throughout the play?

....

....

....

....

TAKING IT FURTHER

Borrowing images

7 Webster not only used a well-known story, but he also borrowed extensively from other writers. Like his contemporaries, he kept a notebook in which he noted down ideas from his reading and play-going.

DC Gunby, in the introduction to the Penguin edition of Webster's plays (1972), analyses one example of a passage [5.5.5–7] that owes much to its source. He points out that Webster probably adapted this from Lavater's *Of Ghostes and Spirites Walking by Night* (1572), in which 'Pertinax for the space of three days before he was slain by a thrust, saw a certain shadow in one of his fishponds, which with a sword ready drawn threatened to slay him, and thereby much disquieted him.'

Look closely at the way in which Webster has used this source and assess whether you think the changes he has made are valuable.

....

....

....

....

Challenge yourself

Another source is Sir Philip Sidney's *Arcadia*. Queen Erona also suffered because she married beneath her, and Sidney writes that in her sorrow one could 'perceive the shape of loveliness more perfectly in woe than in joyfulness'. In Bosola's description of the Duchess, Webster has substituted concrete images of 'tears' and 'smiles', for Sidney's abstract 'woe' and 'joyfulness' [4.1.7–8].

Have you noticed any echoes in Webster's play of passages from earlier poems or plays that you have read? You might, for instance, want to compare the Cardinal's inability to pray with Claudius in Shakespeare's *Hamlet*, or find an echo of the night-time scene between Macbeth and Lady Macbeth after Duncan has been murdered in the tense shared lines between Antonio and Bosola in Act 2 scene 3.

If you have, do you think Webster has merely copied or has he adapted the source material to his play in a manner that enhances it?

Dramatic structure

The five-part structure – originally advocated by Horace in his *Ars Poetica* – was imposed on the play by later editors, not dictated by Webster, although, in the indoor theatre at Blackfriars, there was a need for regular breaks to trim the candles. However, the play does conform to five distinctive phases.

STARTING OUT

'The dramatic arc'

1   The German author and literary critic, Gustav Freytag (1816–1895), having analysed Classical and Renaissance drama, noted that plays usually broke down into five distinct phases. As a result, he developed an analytical tool that is sometimes referred to as the 'dramatic arc'.

Briefly show how the play conforms to the phases identified by Gustav Freytag, shown in the table below. The first is done for you:

ACT 1	Exposition	All main characters are introduced and necessary background information given. The Duchess is in control and takes the initiative by wooing Antonio.
ACT 2	Rising action	
ACT 3	Climax or crisis	
ACT 4	Falling action	

CONTINUED ➔

ACT 5	Dénouement or catastrophe	

Act divisions

2   Consider each of the five acts and explain why each act division is appropriate:

ACTS 1/2	
ACTS 2/3	
ACTS 3/4	
ACTS 4/5	

Alternative analysis of structure

3   An alternative analysis of the structure has been suggested by Professor MC Bradbrook. She suggested that the play falls into five parts, but that the divisions are in different places. She named the parts as shown below. Where would you place the divisions?

PART	DIVISION
The court	
The bedchamber	
The world	
The prison	
The graveside	

KEY SKILLS

Analysing structure

You need to demonstrate an understanding of how the structure of *The Duchess of Malfi* contributes to and influences our understanding of the play as a whole, especially its ideas. For instance, the alternative analysis described previously charts the Duchess' decline from being a powerful ruler, through to becoming a vulnerable woman, then banished, imprisoned and murdered.

Revenge tragedy: a dramatic genre that flourished in the late Elizabethan and Jacobean period, this is a form of tragedy in which the principal theme is revenge and revenge's fatal consequences. However, the term can also be applied to a tragedy in which revenge is an underlying motivation throughout the play.

DEVELOPING YOUR IDEAS

Revenge tragedy

4   Typical ingredients of this genre are in the left-hand column below: in the right-hand column, identify which ones Webster has included and where he has deviated from the norm.

TYPICAL REVENGE TRAGEDY	*THE DUCHESS OF MALFI*
A The hero's quest for vengeance	
B Forbidden love	
C Power struggles	
D The ghost of a murdered kinsman or loved one urging the hero to avenge his death	
E Scenes of real or feigned insanity	
F A play-within-a-play	
G A scene in a graveyard	
H Scenes of carnage and mutilation	
I Infanticide	
J Poisoning	

CONTINUED ➡

Motives for revenge

5   In a revenge tragedy, there is a usually a clear motive for the avenger's actions. It seems that the Cardinal plans his sister's death because, according to his values, she has dishonoured the family name.

As he lies dying, Bosola claims that he acted out of revenge for three murders, two of which he committed, and for his own neglect.

(a) Why do you think Bosola eventually kills the Cardinal and Duke Ferdinand?

....

....

....

(b) Ferdinand has a more obscure but personal motive which he names 'revenge'. Find the following quotations and explore what they reveal about Ferdinand's motives:

QUOTATION	SOURCE
A FERDINAND [to CARDINAL]: I could kill her now / In you, or in myself, for I do think / It is some sin in us heaven doth revenge / By her.	
MOTIVES	
B FERDINAND [to the DUCHESS]: I account it the honorabl'st revenge, / Where I may kill, to pardon. **(pretending to forgive her)**	
MOTIVES	
C FERDINAND [to BOSOLA]: Antonio / Lurks about Milan, thou shalt shortly thither / To feed a fire as great as my revenge, / Which ne'er will slack till it have spent his fuel	
MOTIVES	
D FERDINAND [to BOSOLA]: **(asking why Bosola did not place himself)** Between her innocence and my revenge!	
MOTIVES	

Challenge yourself

Dramatic climax

Where do you consider the play's tragic climax to be located? What is it for you that gives this moment the special quality?

Dumb show

6   What do you think the play gains with the inclusion of the dumb show?

....

....

....

....

....

....

Antimasque

7   In Act 4 scene 2, Bosola orchestrates Ferdinand's campaign to reduce the Duchess to despair. Webster has chosen to structure this as a kind of antimasque, using as a model the elaborate court masques of the period, which were usually designed to celebrate a significant event such as a royal marriage. The elements of a court masque are shown in the left-hand column of the following table. Write in the right-hand column how Webster subverts this:

TRADITIONAL COURT MASQUE	ACT 4 SCENE 2
A Prologue	The madmen
B Presenter	
C Song and dance	
D Presentation of gift to honoured member of audience	
E An epithalamion or formal speech	
F Taking of honoured spectator to join the revels	
G Mood of harmony and peace	

Despair: one of the unforgiveable sins because it signifies that one no longer believes in God's forgiveness.

Masque: a fairly elaborate form of courtly entertainment popular in the reigns of Elizabeth I and James I. The masque combined poetic drama, song, dance and music. The costumes were often sumptuous.

CONTINUED ➡

Madmen

8 Ferdinand expects the madmen to torture the Duchess by depriving her of sleep to bring her to despair, but why do you think Webster included them?

- ● ....

....

- ● ....

....

- ● ....

....

TAKING IT FURTHER

9 Richard Allen Cave writes that this

> grim parody of a wedding masque implies Ferdinand offers it as a sardonic apology for his failure to be present at the Duchess and Antonio's actual ceremony; but it intimates yet more. ... By stylising the tortures into the ritual of the masque Webster allows us to pass through the horror into an awareness of the torment that is riving Ferdinand's soul and sanity apart.
>
> Cave, Richard Allen (1988), *The White Devil and The Duchess of Malfi: Text and Performance*, Basingstoke: Macmillan Education, p. 36.

Do you agree that this scene gives us insights into Ferdinand's mind, or do you think it more likely that it was Bosola who devised the antimasque, and that Webster has given us more insights into the mind of Bosola?

....

....

....

KEY SKILLS

Supporting your argument

You should always support your argument, even if it is based on a critical perspective, through detailed references to the play. You might, for instance, support Cave's opinion by quoting and analysing Ferdinand's response to Bosola's assertion that no one will dare to expose the crime: 'The wolf shall find her grave and scrape it up'.

Challenge yourself

Influences

As his address 'To the Reader' prefaced to *The White Devil* suggests, Webster saw himself as a modern dramatic poet aware of the example of the ancient tragedians and one who particularly 'cherish'd [a] good opinion of other men's worthy labours'.

From your wider reading and theatre-going, can you suggest other plays that seem to have been an influence on Webster in the writing of this play?

TAKING IT FURTHER

10 Webster entitled this play *The Tragedy of the Dutchesse of Malfi*. Below are two definitions of tragedy that were available to him. Read each one and consider how far Webster's play conforms to these definitions:

(a) In the fourth century BC, Aristotle defined tragedy as:

> The imitation of an action that is serious and also, as having magnitude, complete in itself; in language with pleasurable accessories, each kind brought in separately in the parts of the work: in a dramatic, not in a narrative form; with incidents arousing pity and fear, wherewith to accomplish its **catharsis** of such emotions.
>
> Aristotle, *Poetics*

Catharsis: the Greek word for 'purgation'. Aristotle used 'catharsis' to describe the way tragedy, having aroused powerful feelings in the spectator, also has a therapeutic effect; after the storm and climax there comes a sense of release from tension, of calm. Sometimes in the theatre, after a particularly moving tragedy, the audience is absolutely silent for a minute or so, before starting to clap.

Aristotle defined a tragic hero as a man of noble birth with heroic qualities whose fortunes change due to a fatal flaw, 'some error of judgement or frailty', that ultimately brings about the tragic hero's terrible, excessive downfall.

....

....

....

....

....

....

(b) In the sixteenth century, Sir Philip Sidney referred to:

> the high and excellent tragedy, that opens the greatest wounds, and shows forth the ulcers that are covered with tissue; that makes kings fear to be tyrants, and tyrants manifest their tyrannical humours; that with stirring the effects of admiration and commiseration teaches the uncertainty of this world, and upon how weak foundations gilded roofs are builded; that makes us know the savage king who wields the sceptre with cruel sway fears those who fear him; dread comes back to the head of the originator.
>
> Sir Philip Sidney (1579), *An Apology for Poetry* [or *The Defence of Poesy*].

....

....

....

....

....

....

CONTINUED ➡

11 How would you define tragedy for the twenty-first century?

....

....

....

....

....

....

KEY SKILLS

Using terminology

Wherever possible, you should try to include specific and detailed literary terminology in your analysis, therefore remember 'catharsis'.

Themes

A theme in a play is not its subject, but rather one of its central ideas, which may be stated directly or indirectly. The subject of *The Duchess of Malfi* could be said to be revenge, but to identify the themes, we need to decide on the conflicts in the play. Webster asks questions and, if we look carefully, we may be able to find his answers, and therefore the conflicts.

STARTING OUT

Themes overview

1   Complete the spider diagram below to show what you think are the questions at the heart of the play and put arrows between them to show when they are linked. One has been done for you.

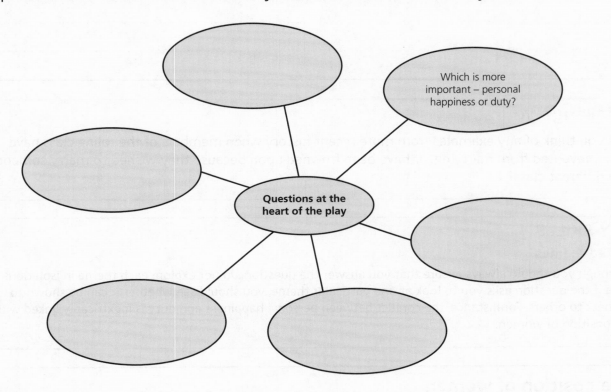

2   Which do you think is the most important theme in *The Duchess of Malfi*? Write a paragraph in which you explain your selection.

I think the most important theme in *The Duchess of Malfi* is ....

....

....

because ....

....

....

....

DEVELOPING YOUR IDEAS

Personal happiness versus duty

3   You may have questioned, as the Duchess herself does, why she should not be allowed to choose her own husband. Gender equality is one of the main concerns for a twenty-first-century audience, so one theme is the conflict between personal happiness and duty.

Why should there be a conflict between personal happiness and duty for the Duchess?

....

....

....

....

....

....

....

Challenge yourself

Can you think of any examples from more recent history when members of the ruling class have been prevented from marrying, or have been frowned upon because they wished to marry someone of a different class?

KEY SKILLS

Linked themes

Although you should always ensure that you answer the question, do not explore each theme in isolation. Even if the question asks you to look at one particular theme, you should see whether it can be shown to connect to others. For instance, the conflict between personal happiness and duty is inextricably linked with the position of women.

The position of women

4   If the Duchess is widowed and in a position of power as ruler of a dukedom, it is difficult for a modern audience to understand why she is still subservient to the authority of her nearest male relatives. A contemporary audience would have taken this for granted, but Webster seems to be questioning the status quo by presenting the Duchess sympathetically.

(a)   What evidence can you find that Webster presents the Duchess sympathetically?

....

....

....

....

....

CONTINUED ➡

Answers can be found at: www.hoddereducation.co.uk/workbookanswers

(b) In Act 2 scene 1, Bosola launches a sustained attack of misogynistic accusations on the Old Lady, yet she is given no opportunity to defend herself. Is this evidence that Webster is also a misogynist?

....

....

....

(c) Julia seems on the surface to conform to a misogynistic stereotype of a loose, over-sexed woman, but do you think Webster's portrayal of her is entirely negative?

....

....

....

....

....

....

Challenge yourself
Shakespeare's spirited heroines

Webster is not the only Renaissance playwright to question the position of women in society. Do you know of any plays by Shakespeare in which spirited heroines defy their male relatives or choose their own husbands by indirect means?

Good government

5   The theme with which Webster opens the play is the question of what constitutes good government. Antonio describes a seemingly idealistic scenario in France, and the rest of the play demonstrates the corruption and oppression which dominates in Italy, although it is generally agreed that Webster is actually writing about the court of King James I.

In the following table, the situation in France is written in the left-hand column; put evidence from Act 1 that shows a different scenario in the courts of Italy.

FRANCE	ITALY
A The king has cleared his court 'Of flatt'ring sycophants, of dissolute / And infamous persons'. [1.1.8–9]	

CONTINUED ➡

FRANCE	ITALY
B The king terms his court 'His Master's masterpiece, the work of heaven'. [1.1.10]	
C The king relies on 'a most provident council, who dare freely / Inform him the corruption of the times'. [1.1.17–18]	

Ambition for worldly glory versus integrity of life

6   Much of the corruption shown in the play stems from ambition for worldly glory, and Webster contrasts this with 'integrity of life', which the final couplet declares is 'fame's best friend'.

(a) What evidence is there that Bosola was corrupted by ambition for worldly glory rather than a desire for money?

....

....

....

....

(b) What evidence is there that Bosola eventually regrets his desire for worldly status?

....

....

(c) What evidence is there that the Cardinal has been corrupted by ambition for worldly glory rather than for reward in heaven?

....

....

(d) What evidence is there that Antonio is aware of the allure of worldly status, but reluctant to give in to ambition?

....

....

....

....

CONTINUED ➡

(e) Explain how the following **sententia** illustrates this theme:

'Glories, like glow worms, afar off shine bright, / But looked to near, have neither heat nor light'.

[4.2.132–133]

....

....

....

(f) Find a quotation that explains what Webster meant by the phrase 'integrity of life'.

....

....

(g) Consider whether the Duchess and Antonio have 'integrity of life'.

....

....

....

....

....

....

Sententia (plural: sententiae): a short pithy statement that expresses an opinion. A successful sententia exposes and condenses an aspect of the truth. Webster frequently presents them as rhyming couplets. In the Methuen edition they are enclosed in quotation marks.

True honour versus 'painted honour'

7 Throughout the play, one of Bosola's preoccupations is with the true nature of honour. Explore this theme in the following quotations:

A	BOSOLA: an honourable pair of crutches [1.1.62]	
B	CARDINAL: No, nor any thing without the addition, honour, / Sway your high blood. [1.1.287–288]	
C	BOSOLA: Can this ambitious age / Have so much goodness in't as to prefer / A man merely for worth, without these shadows / Of wealth and painted honours? [3.2.273–276]	

CONTINUED ➔

D	BOSOLA: poets of your time, / In honour of this trophy of a man / ... Shall thank you, in your grave, for't, and make that / More reverend than all the cabinets / Of living princes. [3.2.288–292]	
E	BOSOLA: Off, my painted honour; [4.2.322]	
F	CARDINAL: I have honours in store for thee. BOSOLA: There are a many ways that conduct to seeming / Honour, and some of them very dirty ones. [5.2.296–298]	

Love and lust

8 To explore the nature of true love, Webster contrasts the relationship between Antonio and the Duchess with that between the Cardinal and Julia. This is made very clear with the juxtaposition at the end of Act 2 scene 3.

Bosola, assuming that the Duchess has a lover because she is pregnant, declares that lust is 'oft found witty, but is never wise'. The dramatic irony is that the audience knows that his accusation is unfounded because the Duchess is married. Webster has carefully alerted us to the contrast between the two women when we hear, at the beginning of the next scene, the Cardinal calling Julia 'a witty false one'.

Juxtaposition: the placing of things next to each other to achieve a particular effect, usually a comparison.

Dramatic irony: when the audience understands the implication and meaning of a situation on stage, or what is being said, but the characters do not.

(a) Fill in the gaps in these quotations:

(i) ANTONIO: Her days are practised in such ....

That sure her nights, nay more, her very sleeps,

Are more .... than other ladies' shrifts.

(ii) DUCHESS: .... and I must tell you,

If you will know where breathes a .... man –

I speak it without .... – turn your eyes

And progress through yourself.

(iii) CARDINAL: Thou art a witty .... one

(iv) CARDINAL: I have taken you off your melancholy ....,

Bore you upon my ...., and showed you ....,

And let you ....

(v) JULIA: .... Now you'll say

I am wanton; this .... in ladies

CONTINUED ➔

> Is but a .... familiar
>
> That .... them.

(b) What does each quotation suggest about the speaker?

(i) ....

....

(ii) ....

....

(iii) ....

....

(iv) ....

....

(v) ....

....

9 You have analysed the characters' use of language; what is there in their behaviour and actions that distinguishes between true love and lust?

- Duchess: ....

....

....

- Antonio: ....

....

....

- Cardinal: ....

....

....

- Julia: ....

....

....

Challenge yourself

Throughout the play, Webster juxtaposes love and death. Look closely at the wooing scene [1.1.351–494] and make a list of all the words associated with agony and death.

KEY SKILLS

Focusing on a passage

Even if the exam question asks you to look at the play as a whole, it can be useful to spend some time in your response focusing on a particular passage. This will help you to demonstrate a detailed appreciation of Webster's skill as a poet and a playwright, as well as specific awareness of how his themes develop within the passage.

Appearance and reality

10 How does Webster explore this theme? Find examples to fit in the grid below:

TECHNIQUE	EXAMPLES
A Through costume	The Cardinal's red robes make him appear to be a holy man of God.
B Through stage directions	
C Through metaphor	
D Through double entendre	
E Through pretence	

Double entendre: the term used to refer to a word or expression so used that it can have two meanings; for example, in Act 1 scene 1 line 314, Ferdinand uses the word 'executed', meaning 'carried out', but he is also implying the other meaning of 'put to death' as a veiled threat.

Challenge yourself

In Act 3 scene 2 lines 273–295, Bosola expresses pleasure and admiration for the Duchess' choice of husband. How far do you think his sentiments are genuine? Can you find any evidence that suggests that Bosola would actually be pleased to see an ordinary man raised up through his own merit?

KEY SKILLS

Analytical sentences

A very important skill for success in exams is to use analytical sentences. There are four elements to an analytical sentence:
1 a quotation or close reference
2 critical terminology
3 an explanation of how the feature has been used
4 an evaluation of what Webster has gained by using it.

Of course, these elements do not all have to be in one sentence, although that will be more succinct. Nor do the four elements have to be in that order; in fact, it is preferable to vary the order.

Answers can be found at: www.hoddereducation.co.uk/workbookanswers

TAKING IT FURTHER

Practise using analytical sentences to explore themes.

11 Fill in the grid to analyse each of the quotations, showing how Webster has used it to explore one of his themes:

QUOTATION OR CLOSE REFERENCE	CRITICAL TERMINOLOGY	EXPLANATION	EVALUATION
A 'a prince's court / Is like a common fountain' [1.1.11–12]	Simile	Just as a poisoned fountain will contaminate the land around,	So a corrupt court will contaminate the whole state.
B 'She stains the time past, lights the time to come.' [1.1.202]	Antithesis		
C 'Keep your old garb of melancholy' [1.1.269]	Metaphor		
D 'This is terrible good counsel.' [1.1.303]	Oxymoron		
E 'Such weddings may more properly be said / To be executed than celebrated.' [1.1.313–314]	Homonym Plosive		

Antithesis: the term used to identify a balanced statement which presents contrasting ideas sharpened by the use of opposite meanings.

Oxymoron: a figure of speech which juxtaposes apparently contradictory words for effect.

Plosive: a plosive consonant is one formed by completely stopping the airflow, so that the sound comes out with a little burst: p/b, t/d, k/g

Challenge yourself

Integrity of life is fame's best friend,
Which nobly, beyond death, shall crown the end.
[5.5.119–120]

This is the sententia with which Webster ends the play. How far do you think this is the moral of the play?

TAKING IT FURTHER

12 Below are several perspectives on the morality of *The Duchess of Malfi*. Think carefully about each one and how it applies to the play. How convincing do you find these ideas about the play's themes? Give each a score out of 10 (10 = most convincing).

DAVID CECIL	Cecil's opinion is that Webster sees the play in religious terms as a conflict between right and wrong, between good and evil.	/10
PETER B MURRAY	Murray feels that Webster accepts that goodness cannot defeat the evil of those who choose to seek for fulfillment in worldly glory. However, Webster offers an alternative way of life in which those who seek happiness in love and caring for others will leave behind a lasting legacy in the memory of others.	/10
PETER MALIN	Malin says that, although Webster gives his audience the anti-Catholic prejudice prevalent at the time of writing, the play is more than an attack on the Catholic Church. He believes that Webster is concerned to explore the nature of truly 'religious' behaviour.	/10
IAN JACK	Jack thinks that Webster is very pessimistic about the human condition. His opinion is that Webster's plays are so sensational and so full of horrors that they demonstrate that the playwright believed there is no moral order. His play portrays a world in which the relationships between God and man, between the individual and society, have been overthrown.	/10
SANDRA CLARK	Clark's opinion is that instead of defining evil in relation to goodness or balanced against opposing forces, Webster sees evil as omnipresent in the world and therefore impossible to defeat.	/10
RUPERT BROOKE	[In] Webster's universe. Human beings are writhing grubs in an immense night. And the night is without stars or Moon. But it has sometimes a certain quietude in its darkness; but not very much. Rupert Brooke, (1916), *John Webster and the Elizabethan Drama*, New York: John Lane Co.	/10

Challenge yourself

Annotate the following passage, closely analysing how the imagery illustrates the difference between love and lust:

> BOSOLA: ... The orange tree bears ripe and green fruit and blossoms altogether, and some
>
> of you [women] give entertainment for pure love; but more for more precious reward.
>
> [2.2.13–16]

Characterisation

Webster's source condemned the Duchess; William Painter calls her 'foolish' and condemns her both for marrying beneath her and for pretending to go on a pilgrimage. Webster's main concern, however, is not to present a moral but to explore the psychology of each of his main characters. To do this, he puts them each under pressure to see how they will react. He presents a situation concerning abuses of power – both political and familial – by two powerful men who are violent and ruthless. He explores how both they and their victims develop as their behaviour becomes more extreme over several years.

Character overview

STARTING OUT

Character descriptions

1   Identify which character is referred to in each description below. NOTE: A character may match more than one description.

DESCRIPTION	CHARACTER
A 'His nature is too honest for such business'	
B 'very valiant'	
C 'Some good he hath done.'	
D 'days are practised in such noble virtue'	
E 'He ne'er pays debts'	
F 'the only court-gall'	
G 'did bestow bribes so largely, and so impudently'	
H Has been 'long in France'	
I 'A most perverse and turbulent nature'	
J 'a behaviour so noble / As gives a majesty to adversity'	

Quotations

2   Draw lines to match the quotation with the character who speaks the words.

QUOTATION		CHARACTER
A 'out of brave horsemanship arise the first sparks of growing resolution that raise the mind to noble action.'		Ferdinand
B 'to avoid ingratitude / For the good deed you have done me, I must do / All the ill man can invent.'		Cariola
C 'How tedious is a guilty conscience!'		Bosola
D 'Whether we fall by ambition, blood or lust, / Like diamonds we are cut with our own dust.'		Antonio
E 'I do not like this jesting with religion, / This feigned pilgrimage.'		Duchess
F 'I through frights and threat'nings will assay / This dangerous venture.'		Cardinal

DEVELOPING YOUR IDEAS

Exploring quotations

3   Explain how each of the quotations from **Activity 2** confirms or develops the character.

A   ....
....
....
....
....

B   ....
....
....
....

C   ....
....
....
....
....
....

D   ....
....
....
....
....
....

E   ....
....
....
....
....

F   ....
....
....
....
....

TAKING IT FURTHER

Psychological depth

4   Write one or more paragraphs giving your views on this statement:

In *The Duchess of Malfi*, Bosola is the only character shown to have any psychological depth.

....

....

....

....

....

....

....

....

....

....

....

....

....

....

....

....

....

....

Apportioning responsibility

5   Five characters are involved in the Duchess' death. In the circle below, create a pie chart to help you decide how much responsibility each bears for the Duchess' death: Duke Ferdinand, the Cardinal, Bosola and the executioners.

KEY SKILLS

Characters are fictional constructs

Note that the statement in Activity 4 uses the expression '**shown to have** psychological depth' rather than 'has psychological depth'. Avoid writing about characters as though they were real people. Demonstrate to the examiner that you are aware they are **fictional constructs** by using expressions like 'shown to be', 'presented as', 'constructed as' and 'created to'.

Challenge yourself

Cast the play with your own choice of well-known stage or film actors. Explain your choices.

The Duchess

STARTING OUT

True or false

1 Which **two** of the following statements about the Duchess are not true?

A Webster does not give her a name.

B She has a son by her first husband.

C She is older than Antonio.

D She has a twin brother.

E She was born into the noble house of Aragon.

F She tries to kill one of her brothers

G She confides in her waiting-woman.

H She kneels while she is strangled.

DEVELOPING YOUR IDEAS

The Duchess' stage directions

You will consider the Duchess' characteristic **dialogue** in more detail in Chapter 4 of this workbook. Webster also uses a full range of other dramatic techniques to suggest and develop character, including **implied stage directions**.

2 What do each of the following quotations suggest about the Duchess' character?

A	FERDINAND: You are my sister. / This was my father's poniard: do you see? / I'd be loath to see't look rusty [1.1.320–322]	Webster does not show any reaction from the Duchess. Is she paralysed with fear, or has she learned as a child that the best way to deal with her brother's threats is to ignore them?

CONTINUED

B	BOSOLA: How greedily she eats them! [2.1.146]	
C	DUCHESS: My hair tangles. [3.2.52]	
D	ANTONIO: Do not weep [3.5.78]	
E	DUCHESS: Your kiss is colder / Than that I have seen an holy anchorite / Give to a dead man's skull. [3.5.85–87]	
F	DUCHESS: I am armed 'gainst misery, [3.5.138]	

3   Does 'the spirit of greatness or of woman / Reign most in her'?

(a)   Look at the scene in which the Duchess woos Antonio [1.1.351–494]. How does Webster show her trying to balance her position as Antonio's social superior with her desire to be wooed and won like any other woman?

....

....

....

....

....

....

....

....

....

....

CONTINUED ➡

(b) Look at Act 2 scene 1. How does Webster show the effects of her pregnancy on her personality?

....

....

....

....

....

(c) Look at Act 3 scene 2 lines 1–69. Show how, in this intimate scene, 'the spirit of woman reign[s] most in her', until she sees Ferdinand.

....

....

....

....

....

(d) Look at Act 3 scene 2 lines 141–319. Now that Ferdinand has heard her speak of her husband, does the Duchess allow any signs of weakness to penetrate her defiant exterior?

....

....

....

....

....

....

(e) Looking closely at what the Duchess says, what she does and what others say about her in Act 4, consider whether imprisonment affects the way she feels about herself.

....

....

....

....

....

....

CONTINUED ➡

....

....

....

KEY SKILLS

Writing about implied stage directions

Remember that the characters do not exist solely on the page. They are to be interpreted by actors and performed live on stage. One way you can demonstrate an awareness of this is to consider, where appropriate, how Webster suggests the Duchess' reactions through spoken text and to give consideration to how the play could be performed.

Challenge yourself

An actress' opinion

Harriet Walter wrote that

Whether the Duchess is selfish, reckless and over-sexed, or on a mission of piety and integrity is not the point. Webster seems more concerned to force us to examine the sexual hypocrisy and misogyny lying behind the male rules of society.

White, Martin, ed. (1998), 'Case study: Harriet Walter on playing the Duchess of Malfi', *Renaissance Drama in Action*, London: Routledge, p. 90.

How much support for each of the first two judgements can you find in the text? How far do you agree with Harriet Walter's conclusion?

If you have managed to see a production, how was the Duchess interpreted?

---

4   Find the following lines that show the Duchess hates being deceitful, and explain why she felt she had to be. The first one is done for you:

1.1.431–438	She is forced to woo Antonio because, being lower class, he could never declare his passion for her.
3.2.157–158	
3.2.179–180	

5   How far is the Duchess at fault?

(a)   At Act 1 scene 1 line 323, Ferdinand says that he would have her stop having 'these chargeable revels'. Explain why you think this is or is not a valid criticism.

....

....

....

CONTINUED ➡

....

....

....

(b) How far do you think she is to blame for putting her private happiness before the welfare of the state?

....

....

....

....

(c) Are there any times when she shows poor judgement?

....

....

....

....

TAKING IT FURTHER

The Duchess and sympathy

6   In 1983, critic Lee Bliss asserted that:

> unconcerned with her duchy's political health, the Duchess seeks private happiness at the expense of public stability. As a ruler, she can be no more lauded for the example she sets than her brothers.
>
> Bliss, Lee, (1983), *The World's Perspective: John Webster and the Jacobean Drama*, Hemel Hempstead: Harvester Press, p. 145.

In *The Jacobean Poets* (1894), Edmund Gosse wrote:

> The characterisation of the Duchess, with her independence, her integrity, and her noble yet sprightly dignity, gradually gaining refinement as the joy of life is crushed out of her, is one calculated to inspire pity to a degree very rare indeed in any tragical poetry.

Which view of the Duchess do you agree with more? Where do your sympathies lie? On a separate piece of paper, make notes or a mind map showing your views. Back them up with references to the text.

Antonio

Particularly at the beginning of the play, Webster uses Antonio as a choric voice, to comment on a range of social issues. This does not really fit with the story as he is supposed to have been out of the country for a long time. However, this does give us insights into Antonio's character.

1   Complete the spider diagram below to show what you know about Antonio. Include quotations and your own words and phrases. Two examples have been provided.

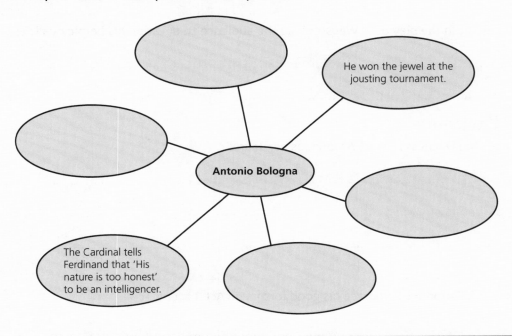

He won the jewel at the jousting tournament.

Antonio Bologna

The Cardinal tells Ferdinand that 'His nature is too honest' to be an intelligencer.

DEVELOPING YOUR IDEAS

Antonio as hero

2 (a)   Write down the qualities that you think a hero should have.

- ....

- ....

- ....

- ....

(b)   What evidence can you find that Antonio has any of these qualities?

- ....

....

- ....

....

- ....

....

CONTINUED ➔

- ....
  ....
  ....
- ....
  ....
  ....
- ....
  ....

(c) At what point in the play does Webster lead the audience to question his heroic qualities?

....

....

The 'laurel' withers

3 (a) Why does the Duchess refer to Antonio as her 'laurel'?

....

....

....

....

(b) How eager is Antonio to embrace his good fortune in Act 1 scene 1?

....

....

....

(c) When the Duchess goes into labour, how does Antonio respond to the emergency?

....

....

....

(d) In Act 2 scene 2, Antonio shows sympathy with the Duchess, but he is preoccupied with his own danger. How do you explain this?

....

....

....

CONTINUED ➡

Answers can be found at: www.hoddereducation.co.uk/workbookanswers

(e)   What clues can you find in the text to suggest how the actor should play Act 2 scene 2?

....

....

....

....

....

(f)   Why does Antonio not come forward to protect the Duchess when Ferdinand invades her bedchamber and instructs her to kill herself?

....

....

....

....

....

....

(g)   Do you notice any change in Antonio in Act 3 scene 5?

....

....

....

....

....

Dramatic irony

4   How does the audience's knowledge that the Duchess is dead affect our response to Antonio in the final Act?

....

....

....

....

....

....

....

....

....

....

TAKING IT FURTHER

5   Consider whether you think the play is weakened because Antonio is an unsatisfactory hero, or whether it strengthens our admiration and sympathy for the Duchess.

....

....

....

....

KEY SKILLS

Different interpretations of character

In your essays, it is important to show how different interpretations have influenced your ideas about Webster's characterisation (AO5). The different interpretations of Antonio's character will have influenced your opinion of him and his part in the play.

Duke Ferdinand

STARTING OUT

1   Webster has chosen to make Duke Ferdinand and the Duchess twins. (In the 2014 Globe Theatre production, actors were cast for the three siblings who were similar in appearance.) Why do you think he has done so? Do some research into the special relationship between twins and find out the effect on the surviving twin when one twin dies.

....

....

....

DEVELOPING YOUR IDEAS

2   Do you think the fact that they are twins helps to explain some of Ferdinand's behaviour?

....

....

....

3   What evidence can you find to support the theory that Ferdinand's feelings for his sister are sexual rather than fraternal?

- ....

....

- ....

....

- ....

....

- ....

....

Ferdinand's youth

4   The Duchess is a young widow, so it follows that Ferdinand is also young. Have you observed any aspects of his character that could be put down to his youth and inexperience?

- ....

....

- ....

....

- ....

....

- ....

....

- ....

....

CONTINUED ➡

- ....
....

Lycanthropy

5 (a) List the symptoms of this disease as described in the text:

- ....
....

- ....
....

- ....
....

- ....
....

(b) How successfully does Webster prepare the audience for Ferdinand's eventual retreat into this type of madness?

....

....

....

....

....

....

....

(c) Ferdinand's speech and behaviour is often horribly funny. If the audience laughs, does it detract from the horror?

....

....

....

....

....

Bosola

In Webster's source, Bosola only comes in at the end of the story. He is the assassin hired to kill Antonio, and he escapes immediately afterwards. Bosola is entirely Webster's creation and, although he bases his character on the stock character of a malcontent, Bosola is much more complicated than this suggests. We learn from Delio that, even at university, Bosola was putting on an act, pretending to be a 'fantastical scholar' in order to gain the reputation of a 'speculative man'.

Malcontent: in late Elizabethan and Jacobean drama, a malcontent stands outside the action to a certain extent, making frequent asides to the audience, and cynically exposing the vices and follies of a society he or she despises, but in which he or she longs to be promoted. He or she is characterised by having a melancholy temperament.

True or false

1   There are similarities between Bosola and Antonio. Which of the following statements is not true?

A Both are commoners.

C Both are attractive to women.

B Both are well educated.

D Both are valiant soldiers.

E Both enjoy intrigue.

G Neither is a flatterer.

F Both are critical of hypocrisy.

DEVELOPING YOUR IDEAS

The only court-gall

2   Bosola was a university scholar, therefore highly educated. What went wrong? Why is he now known as 'the only court-gall' instead of a scholar?

....

....

....

....

Providing evidence

3   In the first half of the play, Bosola's character is established. Fill in the following chart with observations or quotations from the text:

CHARACTER TRAIT	EVIDENCE
A Bosola is witty.	
B Bosola despises flatterers.	
C He speaks bluntly.	
D He wants to be a good man.	
E He is ambitious and willing to do anything for advancement.	
F He enjoys the challenge of finding out the Duchess' secrets.	
G He is the sort of man in whom a woman feels she can safely confide her secrets.	

Bosola's emotional conflict

4   Once he is in possession of her secret, Bosola has a choice to make. Should he be loyal to the Duke or the Duchess? His speeches reveal that he acts against his better nature. Identify quotations that reveal this emotional conflict.

EMOTIONAL CONFLICT	QUOTATION
A He despises himself for being a spy, but still feels obligated to obey Ferdinand.	
B Bosola admires the way the Duchess conducts herself in captivity.	

 CONTINUED

Answers can be found at: www.hoddereducation.co.uk/workbookanswers

C	When the Duchess begins to despair, Bosola tries to comfort her.	
D	Courageously, he does try to prevent Ferdinand from inflicting any more cruelty on his sister.	
E	When Ferdinand insists, Bosola is very reluctant to continue.	
F	Bosola coldly and callously orders the deaths of Cariola and the children.	
G	When Ferdinand refuses to reward him, Bosola regrets his actions.	
H	As he lies dying, he lists his motives for killing the Cardinal and Ferdinand, ending on probably the most cogent reason.	

TAKING IT FURTHER

5   Bosola is a very complex character, open to interpretation by the actor. Consider the following dilemmas:

(a) In Act 3 scene 2, Bosola praises Antonio to the Duchess, even though Antonio appears to be in disgrace. This must be a ploy to gain the Duchess' trust and learn her secrets, but how far do you think his praise is genuine?

....

....

....

(b) When the Duchess confirms that Antonio is her husband, Bosola appears surprised and pleased that a man can be rewarded on merit alone [3.2.273–276]. What evidence can you find in the play that his pleasure is genuine?

●   ....

....

●   ....

....

●   ....

....

CONTINUED ➡

(c) In Act 3 scene 5 line 107, Bosola reassures the Duchess that her brothers mean 'safety and pity'. Do you think that, at this point in the play, he might believe this?

....

....

....

(d) In Act 4 scene 1, how sincere do you think Bosola is when he tries to comfort the Duchess saying he will save her life and he pities her?

....

....

....

(e) After the Duchess curses the stars, Bosola tells her 'the stars shine still'. Do you think he is cynically stressing human fallibility, pointing out that her curse is impotent, or is he reminding her of the permanence of a divine order in which she can put her trust?

....

....

....

(f) Do you think Bosola is deluding himself when he declares that his part in the deaths of the Duchess, Antonio and Julia was 'Much 'gainst mine own good nature' [5.5.85]?

....

....

....

Challenge yourself

In 1962, Irving Ribner wrote: 'Her [The Duchess'] death had been his [Bosola's] regeneration.' Ribner, Irving (1962), *Jacobean Tragedy: The Quest for Moral Order*, London: Methuen, p. 135.
This is a very thought-provoking essay; how far do you agree with Ribner that Bosola is transformed by the Duchess' death into an instrument of justice?

The Cardinal

1 (a)   Complete the spider diagram below showing what sins and crimes the Cardinal is guilty of.

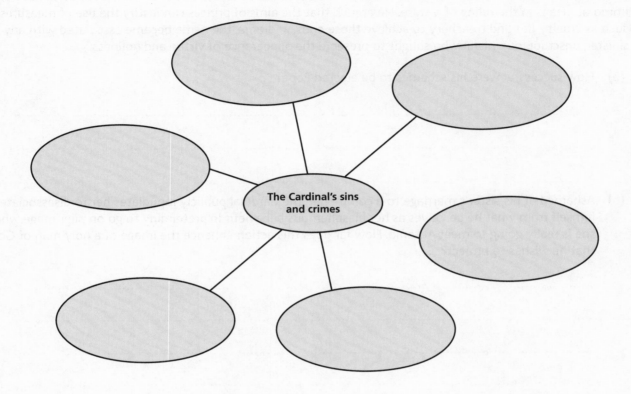

(b)   Explore in detail the one crime or sin that you think is the worst.

....

....

....

....

....

....

....

....

DEVELOPING YOUR IDEAS

The Cardinal as Machiavel

Machiavel: the Cardinal is a 'Machiavel', a stock character from Elizabethan and Jacobean drama. The name derives from Niccolò Machiavelli (1469–1527), whose treatise on statecraft, *Il Principe*, justified the use of immoral means in the ruling of a state. He argued that the aims of princes can justify the use of measures such as cruelty, lies and treachery to achieve those ends. In drama, the name became associated with any sinister, unscrupulous villain who sought to preserve the appearance of virtue and holiness.

2 (a) How successful were his schemes to be elected Pope?

....

....

....

(b) Ashamed of his sister's marriage to a commoner, the Cardinal publicly repudiates her to disassociate himself from what he perceives as her blasphemous behaviour in pretending to go on pilgrimage when she is really going to meet Antonio. How far does this action enhance the image of a holy man of God that he wishes to project?

....

....

....

....

....

....

(c) When asked by Pescara what has happened to make Ferdinand go mad, the Cardinal makes up a story of an apparition who appears to members of their family shortly before they die. What impression of the Cardinal will the audience gain from this story?

....

....

....

(d) The Cardinal's murder of Julia was clearly premeditated as the Bible was already poisoned. How clearly do you think he had thought through his plan?

....

....

....

CONTINUED ➡

Answers can be found at: www.hoddereducation.co.uk/workbookanswers

(e) Why does nobody come to help the Cardinal when Bosola attacks him?

....

....

(f) How does Bosola learn that the Cardinal intends to kill him?

....

....

....

TAKING IT FURTHER

3   What reaction do you think Webster was hoping to achieve from the audience when he planned the Cardinal's death?

....

....

....

....

....

....

....

....

....

Challenge yourself

Delio and Antonio describe the Cardinal at some length in Act 1 scene 1 lines 148–160. Why do you think Webster gives so much detail at the beginning rather than letting the Cardinal's true nature be revealed gradually?

Minor characters

1   Who speaks the following lines?

(a) 'Integrity of life is fame's best friend, / Which nobly, beyond death, shall crown the end.'

(b) 'who would have thought / So great a lady would have matched herself / Unto so mean a person?'

(c) 'Whether the spirit of greatness or of woman / Reign most in her, I know not, but it shows / A fearful madness.'

(d) 'It is fitting a soldier arise to be a prince, but not necessary a prince descend to be a captain.'

(e) 'I go I know not whither.'

DEVELOPING YOUR IDEAS

2   Identify the function(s) of each of these minor characters. The first one is done for you:

CHARACTER	FUNCTION
A Delio	As Antonio's friend and confidante, Delio gives Webster the opportunity to give the audience important information at the beginning of Acts 1, 3 and 5. He is not merely a tool to allow dissemination of information; he takes the initiative and advises Antonio when the latter is at a loss what to do.

Acting against Antonio's dying words, Delio provides hope for the future in the person of Antonio's son. However, as he says 'Let us … join all our force', it sounds as if he is expecting war, presumably against the Duchess' older son.

He is also a more rounded personality in that he is shown trying unsuccessfully to seduce a married woman by offering her money, or he may be trying to use her to spy for Antonio. |
| B   Cariola | |

CONTINUED ➡

CHARACTER	FUNCTION
C Julia	
D Castruchio	
E Pilgrims	

TAKING IT FURTHER

3 If you were directing this play, are there any of these minor characters you might consider omitting from the script? Explain your reasons.

....

....

....

....

....

....

....

....

....

Challenge yourself

The play has often been criticised because the Duchess dies at the end of Act 4, and Act 5 is considered to be an anticlimax. Do you think a more appropriate title for this play would have been *The Malcontent* or *The Tragedy of Daniel de Bosola*?

Writer's methods: Form, structure and language

Writing plays is a craft, and the examiners will expect you to understand the tools Webster had at his disposal, and to appreciate the skill with which he uses them. The following exercises will help you to appreciate what these tools are, as well as how and why he chooses them. Webster's actors were all men and not very highly regarded in society, so you need to explore how his use of form, stagecraft and language help them to sustain the illusion that they are dukes or duchesses, cardinals or common soldiers.

Form

Like his contemporaries, Webster wrote much of his play in **blank verse**, harnessing the natural stress patterns of words to create a rhythmic language. However, the examiners will not be impressed if you just tell them this. If the whole play were in blank verse it would sound very monotonous, so Webster plays with the verse to achieve particular effects. The best approach is to show your knowledge and understanding of the form by exploring how and why he deviates from the basic iambic rhythm.

> **Blank verse**: when not writing in prose, Webster writes in blank verse, i.e. unrhymed iambic pentameters. There are ten syllables per line consisting of five iambic feet: ~ / ~ / ~ / ~ / ~ /. At strategic points, he uses rhyming couplets.

KEY SKILLS

Identifying stress patterns

Poets harness the natural stress pattern of language, easily seen in the different forms of the word 'photograph'. The basic noun has a stressed syllable followed by two unstressed ones: /~~. If we add a 'y' on the end (photography) the pattern changes to ~/~~. If we turn it into an adjective (photographic), the pattern changes again: ~~/~.

Poets create patterns by using repetition. Each repeated pattern is called a 'foot', and there is a different name for each pattern.

STARTING OUT

Verse

1   Identify the stress pattern in the following quotation by marking the stressed and unstressed syllables. The first line has been done for you:

Consid'ring duly that a prince's court   ~ / ~ / ~ / ~ / ~ /

Is like a common fountain, whence should flow   ....

Pure silver drops in general, but if't chance   ....

Some cursed example poison't near the head, ...

Death and diseases through the whole land spread.   ....

[1.1.11–15]

KEY SKILLS

Using literary terminology

Weave your identification of a technique into the sentence in which you analyse its effect. For instance: 'Webster gives Antonio a **rhyming couplet** as he summarises his theme in an extended metaphor, with an end-stopped line followed by an **inverted iambic foot**, laying emphasis on "death".'

Elision: to keep the rhythm, Webster expects the actor to slur certain syllables. This is generally marked by apostrophes to indicate the omission of a sound to create metrical regularity.

Enjambment: Sometimes Webster does not expect the actor to stop at the end of a line, but runs the line on into the next.

Inverted iambic foot: This feature is often to be found at the beginning of a line. It lays extra emphasis on important words and may be used to show that the speaker is disturbed.

Rhyming couplet: When a playwright wants to sum up one of his themes in a memorable form, he may use a rhyming couplet.

Plosives: Another way of laying emphasis and conveying some negative emotion like disgust is to use hard consonants, created by stopping the airflow and releasing it suddenly.

Caesura: a deliberate break or pause in a line of poetry, signified by punctuation.

DEVELOPING YOUR IDEAS

Close analysis

2   The passage in **Activity 1** is a useful one to illustrate some of the methods by which Webster stops his verse sounding monotonous and enables the actor to lay emphasis on particular words. Using the key terms above, explain what Webster was trying to achieve in this passage, paying particular attention to the effect achieved when he deviates from the iambic rhythm.

....

....

....

....

....

....

Shared lines

3   Another way of disguising the verse form is to have characters share a line. This is usually indicated by the way the lines are set out on the page. However, Webster achieves more than mere variety; he uses this feature to indicate mood and emotion. Consider each of the following lines and how you would direct actors to speak them:

    (a) DUCHESS: I'll never marry
         CARDINAL: So most widows say,

[1.1.293]

 CONTINUED

....

....

(b) ANTONIO: And may our sweet affections, like the spheres,
　　　　Be still in motion –
　　　　DUCHESS:　　　　　Quickening, and make
　　　　The like soft music –
[1.1.470–472]

....

....

(c) BOSOLA: And two sweet children –
　　　　ANTONIO:　　　　　　　　　　Their very names
　　　　Kindle a little life in me –
　　　　BOSOLA:　　　　　　　Are murdered!
[5.4.58–59]

....

....

Pauses

4　Using blank verse allows Webster to indicate when he wishes the actor to pause. Analysis of these pauses gives good opportunities to offer different interpretations (AO5). What do you think the characters are thinking when they pause in the following lines? Can you suggest more than one possibility?

QUOTATION	INTERPRETATION
A FERDINAND: Do not ask then. [3.1.83]	
B DUCHESS: 'Tis welcome: [3.2.68]	
C BOSOLA: This is manly sorrow: [4.2.347]	

CONTINUED ➡

QUOTATION	INTERPRETATION
D CARDINAL: Oh justice! [5.5.53]	

Soliloquies and asides

5 Traditionally, characters are being honest in soliloquies because they are thinking aloud or confiding in the audience, and not putting on an act for any other character. This means that they are very important for interpreting character.

(a) The Duchess has only one soliloquy [1.1.331–339] as she is plucking up the courage to ask Antonio to marry her. Do you think this speech helps the audience to empathise with her?

....

....

....

....

....

(b) Cariola has a short soliloquy at the end of Act 1 and Delio at the end of Act 2 scene 4. What do you think is Webster's intention with these speeches?

....

....

....

....

....

....

(c) The Cardinal has an aside at Act 5 scene 2 lines 101–105 and another at Act 5 scene 2 lines 218–222 and two soliloquies at Act 5 scene 4 lines 22–31 and Act 5 scene 5 lines 1–7. Explore what Webster has achieved by giving him soliloquies in the final act.

....

....

....

CONTINUED ➡

....
....
....
....
....
....

(d) Bosola has most of the soliloquies and asides, and this gives him a special relationship with the audience. However, can we always believe that he is being honest when he speaks to the audience? Some of the time, when he talks to the audience, there are other characters on stage. This leads to ambiguity, as we cannot tell whether he is expecting to be overheard. At the end of Act 5 scene 4, he seems to soliloquise, even though there is a servant on stage who might report his threat to the Cardinal. Did he pretend remorse to fool the servant? Is the 'direful misprision' the fact that he killed Antonio or that he failed to kill the Cardinal?

Look closely at the language of his soliloquy at the end of Act 5 scene 2 and explore the ambiguity:

....
....
....
....
....
....
....
....
....
....

Challenge yourself

Antonio has no soliloquies, just a few asides showing his nervousness while the Duchess is in labour. Do you think the resignation he shows to his wife in Act 3 scene 5 lines 69–80 and the optimism he shows to Delio in Act 5 scene 1 reflect his true feelings? Write a soliloquy for Antonio in which he shows the audience the conflicting emotions that trouble him. Try writing in blank verse; it is not as difficult as you might think and will help you to appreciate the craft of the poet.

Dramatic irony

6   The audience is privy to much more information than any of the characters, and Webster uses dramatic irony with great skill to increase the suspense.

(a) In which scenes do you think Webster uses dramatic irony most effectively to increase the tension for the audience and keep them on the edge of their seats?

- ....

  ....

- ....

  ....

- ....

  ....

(b) At other times, the dramatic irony can lead to comedy. Can you think of any times when you were tempted to laugh because you had knowledge that the characters were not privy to?

- ....

  ....

  ....

- ....

  ....

(c) Sometimes, as you hear the actor speak one of Webster's sententiae or aphorisms, the audience – with its greater knowledge – realises that the character is vainly seeking comfort and security in proverbial wisdom. Explain how the Duchess is seeking comfort in the following aphorism: 'There's no deep valley, but near some great hill' [3.5.140].

....

....

KEY SKILLS

Using more than one quotation

It may be appropriate to find more than one piece of evidence or quotation to support the point you are making. A quotation can be as short as one word, if it is well chosen.

Sententiae

7   Complete the following sententiae and name the speaker:

(a) 'They pass through whirlpools, and deep woes do shun, / Who the event weigh,

....,'

Speaker: ....

(b) 'That friend a great man's ruin strongly checks, / Who rails into his belief,

....,'

Speaker: ....

(c) 'We value not desert, nor Christian breath, / When we know black deeds must

....,'

Speaker: ....

(d) 'Integrity of life is fame's best friend, /

....,'

Speaker: ....

Antithesis and chiasmus

8   Another form Webster uses to draw attention to a statement is to give it balance. In the following example of **chiasmus**, Webster contrasts 'soldier' with 'captain', and 'arise' with 'descend', but he reverses the order, like a see-saw, using 'but' as the pivot. This makes the statement sound like a truism.

> CASTRUCHIO: It is fitting a soldier arise to be a prince, but not necessary a prince descend to be a captain.
>
> [1.1.93–94]

Why do you think Webster has drawn attention to this opinion?

....

....

....

....

....

> Chiasmus: A particular type of antithesis in which a balanced statement is constructed rather like a see-saw; a grammatical structure is reversed to point out the contrast between the words.

TAKING IT FURTHER

9   In Webster's day, a young man would have played the Duchess. Scan the following speech and analyse the ways in which Webster has used the poetic form to help him sound like a woman who is about to give birth.

> I think she did – come hither, mend my ruff,
> Here, when? Thou art such a tedious lady –
> And thy breath smells of lemon peels – would thou hadst done –

CONTINUED ➡

Shall I swoon under thy fingers? I am
So troubled with the mother.
[2.1.109–113]

....

....

....

....

....

Setting and staging

We have looked at the broad dramatic structure in Chapter 1, but examiners also reward close detailed analysis of Webster's 'dramaturgical skills': sets, lighting, sound effects and music, stage properties, etc. Webster exploits all of the styles and dramatic forms available to a Renaissance dramatist: darkness, disguises, overhearing, children, a dumb show, madmen, corpses on stage, etc. You have been given the text to study, but to appreciate the play, you need to appreciate the alchemy of bringing together the text, the actors and the stagecraft.

Challenge yourself

Below are the opinions of two critics. At this stage in your study, which one do you most agree with?

William Archer (1893)	DC Gunby (1972)
When we find a playwright … drenching the stage with blood even beyond the wont of his contemporaries and searching out every possible circumstance of horror – ghosts, maniacs, severed limbs, and all the paraphernalia of the charnel-house and the tomb – with no conceivable purpose except just to make our flesh creep, may we not reasonably … conclude that he either revelled in 'violent delights' for their own sake, or wantonly pandered to the popular craving for them. Archer, William (1893), 'Webster, Lamb, and Swinburne', *News Review*.	In the introduction to the Penguin edition of Webster's plays, DC Gunby expressed the opinion that Webster wants to instruct his audience as well as entertain them. He praises Webster as a great poet and dramatist with a deep and rich tragic vision as well as the skills to present his vision. Gunby sees Webster as offering answers to the spiritual problems of the early-seventeenth century. He says that Webster's proud characters are brought to humility and self-knowledge; those of his characters who seek worldly glory are disillusioned. In Gunby's opinion, Webster is not merely a didactic writer, but a poet and a playwright of exceptional skills who manages to create highly subtle and coherent works of art, offering a complex, moving and deeply religious vision of existence.

STARTING OUT

Settings

Elizabethan and Jacobean theatres did not have elaborate stage sets, so Webster does not give much direction as to the setting. This means that it is not clear where some of the scenes are set. Is the Duchess, for instance, imprisoned in her palace or in a dungeon? Does it matter? What is important is that the setting is dark and sinister where necessary. Webster's language had to create the atmosphere and compensate for the lack of sets.

CONTINUED ➡

Answers can be found at: www.hoddereducation.co.uk/workbookanswers

1 (a) Where does he use the 'traverse' or 'arras', a curtain concealing the recess at the back of the stage?
Who or what is hidden behind the curtain?

- ....

- ....

- ....

(b) Where does he use the minstrel's gallery above the stage?

....

Stage props

2 (a) Costumes would have been very sumptuous, helping poor actors give the illusion that they were
princes, and Webster does specify some essential stage props. Jot down as many as you can
remember:

ACT 1	ACT 2	ACT 3	ACT 4	ACT 5

(b) Look through the text and choose six of the props. Describe below why these props are essential.

- ....

....

- ....

....

- ....

....

- ....

....

- ....

....

CONTINUED ➡

Stage directions

3   Remind yourself of Act 4 scene 2 and note Webster's stage directions. Remember that sometimes he uses implicit stage directions in the speeches of his characters. How successful do you think this scene would be if the actors followed the stage directions and acted it as a dumb show?

....

....

....

....

DEVELOPING YOUR IDEAS

Stage effects

4   How do darkness and stage effects heighten the tension in the following scenes?

   (a)   Act 2 scene 3: ....

   ....

   ....

   (b)   Act 5 scene 4: ....

   ....

   ....

Music

5   Webster gives quite specific instructions for the use of music. How does this contribute to the impact of the action on stage in each of the following scenes?

STAGE DIRECTION	EFFECT
A 'this ditty is sung to very solemn music' [3.4]	
B 'this song is sung to a dismal kind of music' [4.2]	

CONTINUED

Answers can be found at: www.hoddereducation.co.uk/workbookanswers

C	*'Here the dance consisting of eight madmen, with music answerable thereunto'* [4.2]	
D	*'Enter* EXECUTIONERS *with a shrouded coffin, cords and a bell'* [4.2]	

Distancing

If you look closely, you will see that Webster is controlling the action rather like a rider directing a horse. It would be very easy to let the action speed towards its horrible conclusion, but Webster employs strategies to slow down the pace before building up the menace to be more intense, like a rider reining in the horse before a jump. When the Duchess is arrested in Act 3 scene 5, Webster gives her a long speech as she tells Bosola a fable in which the fisherman represents God and the fish market is the Last Judgement. With this illustration of the moral that 'Men oft are valued high, when th'are most wretched' [3.5.38], Webster pauses the action before a harrowing scene.

6   Analyse the echo scene [5.3] closely to explore how effectively Webster distances the menace after Julia is poisoned, and slows the action before the final dénouement.

....

....

....

....

....

....

....

....

TAKING IT FURTHER

7   Having done the close detailed analysis suggested in these questions, look back at the views of William Archer and DC Gunby, and consider whether your attitude to the staging of this play has changed.

....

....

CONTINUED ➡

....

....

....

....

....

....

Language

STARTING OUT

When I saw another production of the play, after I had finished my own production, I saw how little of the play's impact depends on the tying up of loose ends. The language of the play is its strength, it seems to me. Surrender to the sensation of that dark language (as actor or audience) and one understands with the instinct, the imagination and the emotional memory, and in this way one comes closer to the essence of the play than ever one can by intellect alone.

White, Martin, ed. (1998), 'Case study: Harriet Walter on playing the Duchess of Malfi', *Renaissance Drama in Action*, London: Routledge, p. 89.

1 How much of 'that dark language' lingers in your memory? Without looking at the text, jot down any images or phrases which have had a significant effect on you. Spend a little while on this exercise and you will be surprised how much you eventually remember:

DEVELOPING YOUR IDEAS

Patterns of imagery: birds

2 (a) In order to illuminate the themes of his play, Webster develops patterns of imagery by using images from carefully chosen semantic fields. You might have noted one or more of the references to birds. How many can you find?

- ....
- ....
- ....
- ....
- ....
- ....
- ....

(b) The only actual bird in the play is the owl that screamed while the Duchess was in labour [2.3.7–9]. Usually, Webster uses them metaphorically. What do each of the birds you found represent?

- ....
- ....
- ....
- ....
- ....
- ....
- ....

Patterns of imagery: animals

3 (a) Another pattern Webster uses is from the animal world. Fill in the gaps in the following quotations:

(i) ANTONIO: The spring in his face is nothing but the engend'ring of ....
[1.1.152]

(ii) DELIO: The law to him

Is like a foul black .... to a ....
[1.1.170–171]

(iii) ANTONIO: I would this terrible .... would come again
[3.2.146]

(iv) DUCHESS: Go tell my brothers when I am laid out,

They then may .... in quiet.
[4.2.222–224]

CONTINUED ➡

(v) DOCTOR: ... he howled fearfully;

Said he was a ...., only the difference

Was, a .... skin was hairy on the outside,

His on the inside;
[5.2.15–18]

(vi) CARDINAL: Shall I die like a ....

Without any resistance?
[5.5.43–44]

(vii) FERDINAND: Give me some wet hay, I am ....

I do account this world but a ....
[5.5.65–66]

(b) Consider how creating a pattern of imagery in this way helps to illuminate one of Webster's themes.

....

....

....

....

....

....

....

....

Patterns of imagery: water

4 (a) Fill in the gaps in these quotations:

(i) ANTONIO: .... a prince's court

Is like a common ....
[1.1.11–12]

(ii) BOSOLA: He and his brother are like plum trees that grow crooked over

....:
[1.1.48–49]

(iii) BOSOLA: .... an honest statesman to a prince

Is like a cedar planted by a ....;
[3.2.259–260]

CONTINUED

Answers can be found at: www.hoddereducation.co.uk/workbookanswers

(b) Consider how creating a pattern of imagery in this way helps to illuminate one of Webster's themes.

....

....

....

....

....

....

TAKING IT FURTHER

5 Find examples of imagery that explores another of Webster's themes, and show how the theme is developed through his choice of imagery. You may like to research images of disease and decay, the theatre, precious stones, etc.

THEME:	
Examples of imagery	**Development of theme**

Challenge yourself

Webster's imagery

According to Hereward Price, Webster's imagery 'is the most pregnant expression of truth. It reveals character, it does the work of argument, it emphasises mood, and it prefigures the events to come' Price, Hereward (Hunter GK ed.) (1969), 'The Function of Imagery in Webster', *John Webster: A Critical Anthology*, London: Penguin, p. 179. How far do you agree with this view? Find examples to illustrate each of the roles that Price thinks are fulfilled by the imagery in this play.

Playing on words

6 (a) Sometimes, Webster's characters use puns for comic effect, to create a playful mood or to show the Duchess' strength. Fill in the gaps in the following quotations and make sure you understand the play on words:

    (i) DUCHESS: Oh, you are an .... treasurer
        [1.1.362]

        Meaning of pun: ....

    (ii) DUCHESS: St Winifred, that were a strange ....!

        ANTONIO: 'Twere strange if there were no .... in you

        To marry again.
        [1.1.380–381]

        Meaning of pun: ....

    (iii) CARIOLA: Wherefore still when you lie with my lady

        Do you .... so early?
        [3.2.16–17]

        Meaning of pun: ....

    (iv) DUCHESS: Let me be a little merry. Of what stuff wilt thou make it?

        BOSOLA: Nay, resolve me first, of what ....?

        DUCHESS: Why, do we grow fantastical in our death-bed, do we affect

        .... in the grave?
        [4.2.139–142]

        Meaning of pun: ....

  (b) Sometimes Webster uses a pun for the audience to pick up on, but the character who speaks it is not aware of the second meaning, and so the polysemy helps to create tension:

    (i) DUCHESS: So now the ground's broke

        You may discover what a wealthy ....

        I make you lord of.
        [1.1.417–419]

    (ii) DUCHESS: … here upon your lips

        I sign your ....
        [1.1.453–454]

Polysemy: deliberate play on words that have more than one meaning. A pun is an example of polysemy which the character uses deliberately.

           Answers can be found at: www.hoddereducation.co.uk/workbookanswers

TAKING IT FURTHER

7   Practise writing analytical sentences to explain how Webster has used some of the tools at his disposal. Remember that it does not matter in what order you include the four key elements of the sentence, and you may need two sentences to explain your point fully. Here is an example:

In this example of Webster's use of polysemy, the Cardinal speaks metaphorically of their noble bloodline being tainted by the Duchess' pregnancy; Duke Ferdinand then picks up the word 'blood' and imagines purging her of real blood and thus controlling her passionate nature.

QUOTATION OR CLOSE REFERENCE	CRITICAL TERMINOLOGY	EXPLANATION	EVALUATION

Challenge yourself

A play is created when the text, the staging and the actors come together. Re-read the quotation by Harriet Walter at the beginning of this section, and consider how far you agree with her that the language of the play is its strength, rather than the stage effects which Webster specifies. If you are lucky enough to see a production, perhaps you might find that your opinion changes.

Contexts

In the exam, you will need to demonstrate an understanding of 'the significance and influence of the contexts in which literary texts are written and received' (AO3). You will need to understand and explore contexts such as some aspects of the life of John Webster, attitudes to women and marriage, contemporary theatres and plays, and the reign of James I. However, the examiners do not want you to tack on a paragraph of what you have learned; they want your awareness of the contexts to be integrated into your analysis and exploration of the topic they have set for discussion.

Biographical context

STARTING OUT

Webster was a Londoner, born and brought up amid all the hustle and bustle of the capital city. About 15 years after Shakespeare's birth, Webster was born into a well-off family whose trade was making carriages, carts, etc. It is believed that, in 1598, he went to university – the Middle Temple – one of the four Inns of Court, where he studied Law and met other playwrights. It appears that he failed to finish his course, so he may have been disillusioned with the legal profession. As a playwright, he first collaborated on plays with others, but his first solo play was *The White Devil*, which was first staged in 1612.

English playwrights found drama the perfect medium to express their 'new' ideas and to criticise the 'old' world, which was still the status quo. In medieval theatre, characters represented a single vice or virtue and plots concentrated on the conflict between good and evil. Renaissance playwrights shifted the focus to individual characters, who each had the capacity for both good and evil.

The Law

1   In Act 1 scene 1 lines 166–173, how does Webster use Ferdinand to satirise the legal profession?

....

....

....

....

....

....

....

....

....

....

....

Webster's world: England and London

STARTING OUT

In 1605, three London playwrights – Jonson, Chapman and Marston – were imprisoned for anti-Scottish jokes in the play *Eastwood Ho*. To avoid the strict censorship of the time, Renaissance playwrights often set their plays abroad. Like his contemporaries, Webster uses the distancing of a historical and foreign setting to reflect on social and political issues of his own time and country. Webster holds a mirror up to various facets of contemporary English society.

1   How are the following pieces of context reflected in Webster's play?

(a) Born in the 1570s, Webster grew up during the reign of Queen Elizabeth I, who avoided being under the domination of a man by refusing to marry.

....

....

....

....

(b) Webster's father's coach business was situated just outside London's city wall; nearby were Smithfield market, where executions sometimes took place, St Bartholomew's Hospital, and Newgate Prison. Infant mortality was high and life expectancy low. Almost every year, the plague killed thousands of people.

....

....

....

....

....

(c) For entertainment, Londoners would enjoy laughing at the behaviour of the mad in Bedlam, the Hospital of St Mary of Bethlehem in London.

....

....

....

....

....

....

CONTINUED ➔

(d) Christopher Marlowe, the playwright, was one of many students recruited as a spy while they were at University.

....

....

....

....

(e) England was a Protestant country. The first performance of this play was only nine years after the Catholic plot to blow up the Houses of Parliament was discovered. Protestant orthodoxy presented Catholics as politically and morally corrupt. It was against the law to practise the Catholic religion.

....

....

....

DEVELOPING YOUR IDEAS

Quotations

2   Find quotations you could use in your answers to show the examiner your understanding of each of the previous pieces of context:

(a) ....

....

(b) ....

....

(c) ....

....

(d) ....

....

(e) ....

....

Webster's world: King James I

King James I was widely criticised. He was autocratic and did not listen to his advisers; indeed he did not call a parliament for 11 years, from 1610 to 1621, except for once in 1614 because he needed money. He caused resentment by giving English wealth and offices to his Scottish favourites, who then took their cue from the king by spending colossally more than they could afford. His favourites were pretty boys, not men of sense and good judgement. James was constantly looking for ways to make money to fund his extravagant lifestyle, and so he not only sold titles but also created new titles to sell. This meant that the men in high office were not given their positions on merit, and they were often incompetent and uninterested in government.

A well-run court

1   In 1599, James had written a book for his eldest son, Henry, called the *Basilikon Doron*, or Royal Gift, in which he set out a king's duties and responsibilities. Write a paraphrase of Antonio's speech [1.1.5–22] which reflects the *Basilikon Doron* in its description of a well-run court.

....

....

....

....

....

Not surprisingly, this book was taken as reason to welcome the accession of James to the throne in 1603. However, it soon became apparent that he did not practise what he preached.

A divinely ordained hierarchy

2   James I and the aristocracy claimed a divinely ordained hierarchy, with them at the top. However, in England the reality was that land and wealth was being acquired by commoners such as lawyers, merchants and administrators. Cardinal Wolsey and Thomas Cromwell bear witness to the fact that this had been happening for some time, so the aristocracy were desperate to cling on to their exclusivity.

How is this reflected in Webster's play?

....

....

....

Webster's veiled criticism

3   Find quotations which show how Webster has used his play to criticise the court of King James and expose the hypocrisy behind *Basilikon Doron*:

(a) Among other things, James encouraged his son to be a good king, as opposed to a 'tyrant', by establishing and executing laws, as well as governing with justice and equality.

....

....

(b) In the court and household, he should carefully select loyal gentlemen and servants 'of a good fame and without blemish' to surround him.

....

....

....

(c) James insisted that anything 'spoken in darkenesse, should be heard in the light'.

....

....

....

Poison

Poison was a well-known way of disposing of your enemies. As an example of the scandalous corruption of the court, it is worth noting that, while Webster was writing *The Duchess of Malfi*, the King's favourite was Robert Carr. He was showered with honours, and when he wanted to marry the Countess of Essex, the King colluded to get her an annulment from her husband on the grounds of his impotency due to witchcraft. Thomas Overbury, a former friend of Carr's, disapproved strongly of the marriage and was imprisoned for refusing the King's offer of the post of ambassador to Russia. He died in agony, and, two years later, Carr and his wife were imprisoned for poisoning Overbury. It was also rumoured that Carr poisoned James' son and heir, Henry, in 1612.

4   Explore how Webster uses poison, literally and metaphorically, to explore his theme of the conflict between good government and corruption/oppression:

....

....

....

....

Webster's world: The position of women

Legally, women were under the control of their nearest male relative; however, widows could claim a degree of independence which threatened the male elite. Therefore, the brothers travelled to Malfi to assert their dominance when their sister's husband died. In the *Basilikon Doron*, James says it is his son's 'office to command' his wife, and her duty to 'obey him'. He should 'cherishe her' as his helper, but stop her 'meddling' in politics, leaving her to preside over the 'rule of the house'. The Church supported this position, arguing that Eve had played the principal role in the fall of man.

Contemporary male attitudes

1 (a) Find quotations that reveal the following contemporary male attitudes to women:

(i) Women were thought to have a stronger sexual appetite than men.

....

....

(ii) Because they were sexually experienced, widows were believed to be especially influenced by their libido.

....

....

(iii) Marriage is a union which should be chosen by the family in order to enhance family power.

....

....

(iv) Men expected women to be quiet, not talking very much.

....

....

(b) However, during the Renaissance, an alternative view of marriage emerged. The companionate ideal of marriage placed love and compatibility above the demands of family honour. Write a paragraph considering the ways in which Webster's play supports this companionate ideal.

....

....

....

....

....

....

....

....

Renaissance: from the French for 'rebirth', a cultural movement which began in Italy in the mid-fourteenth century and spread to the rest of Europe by the sixteenth. Renaissance thinkers scoured libraries for works by classical authors, seeking to improve and perfect their worldly knowledge. It was an exciting time of change and upheaval in almost every walk of life, as new thinkers were challenging received opinions.

Challenge yourself
Making the audience aware of the historical context

A modern director is faced with the dilemma of making the audience aware of relevant contexts. Many of these problems centre on social attitudes that are now alien to us:

- the absolute authority of a duke or a cardinal
- the highly stratified society in which marriage between the classes was a shocking and dangerous challenge to the status quo.
- a woman's social position as always subject to her nearest male relative
- the inability of a commoner, however able and admired, to improve his position in society.

What advice would you give to the actors to help them get these attitudes across in the theatre?

DEVELOPING YOUR IDEAS

Witchcraft

In 1597, after being personally involved in witch trials in North Berwick, James I published a book on *Daemonologie*. In this book, he aimed to prove the existence of witchcraft and explain the necessity of persecuting a witch in a Christian society. In 1612, there was a famous witch trial in Lancashire at which ten women were sentenced to hang. One reason why it was usually women who were accused of witchcraft was because solitary women posed a threat to a society in which they were expected to be subordinated to their husband, father or brother.

2 Re-read some of the references to witchcraft in the play, and consider why Webster has included them. Add your explanations below.

EXAMPLES OF WITCHCRAFT	EXPLANATION
A 'For they whose faces do belie their hearts / Are witches ere they arrive at twenty years, / Ay, and give the devil suck.' [1.1.300–302]	
B 'How idly shows this rage, which carries you / As men conveyed by witches through the air / On violent whirlwinds!' [2.5.49–51]	
C Section beginning 'I do suspect there hath been some sorcery / Used on the Duchess.' [3.1.63–78]	

CONTINUED ⊙

Answers can be found at: www.hoddereducation.co.uk/workbookanswers

D	'So you have some virgins / That are witches.' [3.2.139–140]	
E	'What witchcraft doth he practise, that he hath left / A dead man's hand here?' [4.1.53–54]	

KEY SKILLS

Using your contextual knowledge

Referencing contextual factors is only valuable when it genuinely informs your interpretation of *The Duchess of Malfi*. There is no point in including a piece of context for the sake of it. So, if you do write about witchcraft, make sure you show how Webster uses it to build up to Ferdinand's eventual retreat into madness.

TAKING IT FURTHER

3 Write an analytical paragraph demonstrating your knowledge of the position of women in an exploration of the theme of love.

....

....

....

....

....

....

Challenge yourself

Research contemporary theatres

The Duchess of Malfi was first performed privately in 1613–1614 at the indoor Blackfriars Theatre and then later for the general public at the open-air Globe Theatre. Blackfriars was so-called because it had been a Dominican friary until the dissolution of the monasteries in the 1530s; the cloister was on one side of the theatre and the river on the other.

If you cannot get to the reconstructed Globe in London, look for pictures, so that you can imagine the staging of different scenes. There are no pictures of the Blackfriars Theatre, so seek out pictures of performances at the Middle Temple Hall, which will give you some idea of what it was like.

Webster's world: Jacobean theatres

STARTING OUT

Darkness

1   Blackfriars Theatre was lit by candles, and the play is carefully structured with breaks for the candles to be trimmed. Performances at The Globe were staged in the afternoon, using daylight. Remind yourself of those scenes set at night and note below how Webster encourages the audience to imagine that it is night time:

(a)   Act 2 scene 3: ....

....

....

(b)   Act 4 scene 1: ....

....

....

(c)   Act 5 scene 4 lines 42–50: ....

....

....

DEVELOPING YOUR IDEAS

Staging

2   (a)   Who and what hide behind the curtain across the recess at the back of the stage?

....

....

(b)   How was the effectiveness of the echo scene enhanced when staged at Blackfriars Theatre?

....

....

....

....

....

....

KEY SKILLS

Make your own revision cards

Condense your knowledge of each of the contexts into five or six bullet points. Write them onto an A6 card and keep them in your pocket to revise from at any time. It is a good idea to do the same for characters, themes, form, structure and language.

Answers can be found at: www.hoddereducation.co.uk/workbookanswers

Critical approaches

The text in the book is not the play. A play is intended to be performed and only when the text is interpreted by actors, supported by stage crew, costume designers, musicians, etc. does the text become a play. This means that the text is not fixed; different interpretations can be valid.

As you explore different critical approaches, as well as being given fresh ideas about the play, you will come across ideas that will help you gain marks for different interpretations (AO5). You should explore not only the opinions of established critics, but also take on board the views of actors and directors who have studied the play very closely and know what works on stage. It is possible to find interviews on the internet, both written and on film.

Whether or not you are lucky enough to see a stage production, it is a good idea to watch one of the productions available on DVD or the internet.

STARTING OUT

Reading reviews

1   In the following table are some comments from critics of actual performances. How important do you think are the points they make about the play?

CRITIC'S VIEW	YOUR RESPONSE
A The director 'does not wallow in the gore but concentrates on a clear exposition of the machinations of the malicious plotters'. Howard Loxton, Review of the 2010 production at the Greenwich Theatre, London, directed by Elizabeth Freestone, www.britishtheatreguide.info	
B 'In the past, I have found it hard to take seriously the scenes in which he [Ferdinand] torments her [the Duchess] with a dead hand and with waxworks of her supposedly murdered husband and son.' Paul Taylor, 'The Duchess of Malfi, theatre review: "Gemma Arterton is luminous"', Independent, 16 January 2014	
C 'its strong cast and rich costumes helped to deliver quite an effective version of the play.' Rowland Wymer (Sarah Annes Brown, Robert I. Lublin and Lynsey McCulloch eds.) (2013), 'The Duchess of Malfi on Film: Peter Huby's Quietus', Reinventing the Renaissance: Shakespeare and his Contemporaries, Basingstoke: Palgrave Macmillan, p. 272.	

Challenge yourself

Read online some of the reviews about the RSC 2018 production at the Swan Theatre in Stratford. The review by Michael Billington of the *Guardian* points out that the director's intended focus is on 'masculinity and madness'. How much of the play is lost, do you think, when a director focuses on a single theme? How far do you agree that this is Webster's most important theme?

Writing a review

2   Write a review of a production or scene that you have watched. Consider the following points:

● When was the play set? How successful was that with a play intended for a Jacobean theatre and audience?

....

....

● How closely did the production follow Webster's stage directions?

....

....

● Which theme or themes were explored most strongly? How?

....

....

● How successfully did the production balance the comic elements with the tragedy?

....

....

● How convincing and how true to the text did you find the actors?

....

....

DEVELOPING YOUR IDEAS

In the twentieth century, various critical viewpoints emerged which are useful to explore:

Performance criticism

3   Performance criticism considers the text in terms of how meaning is created through the medium of performance. An important aspect of this is whether a production can make the play relevant and accessible to a modern audience, whether or not the cast perform in modern dress.

Thinking of the productions and/or scenes you have watched, did you appreciate them only as visual aids to your revision or were you able to find anything in them that you could enjoy or that gave you food for thought?

....

....

....

Psychoanalytic criticism

4   In 1900, Sigmund Freud published one of the founding texts of psychoanalysis. Psychoanalytic critics see literature as like dreams. Both are fictions, inventions of the mind that, although based on reality, are not literally true. The theory is that much of what lies in the unconscious mind has been repressed or censored by consciousness and emerges only in disguised forms such as dreams or fantasies. This theory could be used to explain Ferdinand's behaviour, as he uses Bosola to act out his obsessive fantasies.

By contrast, Raymond Williams dismissed the implication that Ferdinand was in the grip of a Freudian obsession; he complimented the play's sober recognition of anger, confusion and violence, the ridicule or ritual 'murderously destructive of isolated appetites' (Raymond Williams, *Raymond Williams on Television:*

CONTINUED ➡

Answers can be found at: www.hoddereducation.co.uk/workbookanswers

Selected Writings, Alan O'Connor, ed. (1989), Abingdon: Routledge, p.190.

Which of these two opinions do you find most convincing? Explain your choice.

....

....

....

....

....

Marxist criticism

Political readings of literature focus on social aspects of a text, as opposed to personal or individual factors; they explore a text in terms of the historical circumstances in which it was written. Marxist criticism gives special emphasis to the interactions between social classes.

5   What aspects of the play reflect the socio-political circumstances of Webster's time?

- ....

- ....

- ....

- ....

6   In what ways is the play still relevant to the socio-political circumstances of today's Britain?

....

....

....

....

Challenge yourself

In 1981, John L Selzer wrote:

The Duchess decides to violate degree, not out of weakness or passion or naïveté, but because she wishes, like Webster – to promote in Malfi a new ethic, one rooted in the primacy of worth over degree.

Selzer, JL, 'Merit and Degree in Webster's *The Duchess of Malfi'*, *English Literary Renaissance, Vol. 11, No. 1 (Winter 1981)*, pp. 70–80.

This convincingly argued essay can be read free on the following website, courtesy of the University of Chicago Press Journals: www.jstor.org. (Search for the essay title.)

How far do you agree with Selzer? Can you find any evidence in the play for his viewpoint?

Feminist criticism

Feminist criticism challenges assumptions about gender and exposes sexual stereotyping. There has been much debate about whether Webster endorses the status quo of the patriarchal society or whether he has feminist sympathies.

7   It was the Duchess' womanhood that brought her down because her pregnancy alerted her enemies. Do you think Webster is saying that it was inevitable that a woman who challenged male superiority would end up a victim? Use evidence from the text to support your answer.

....

....

....

....

8   Is Julia a victim or a strong feminist who has to work within the patriarchal system, which gave her to an impotent husband, to pursue her own path, confidently choosing her own lovers? Do you see her death as pathetic or would you agree that she died faithful to the way she lived?

....

....

....

....

9   Consider the two viewpoints below. Which of them do you think more accurately reflects the mood of the play?

   A   All three female characters die as a result of their attempts to evade or subvert the male order. In the final dénouement, there are no women left, so Webster is suggesting that women will never be able to successfully challenge and overcome male rule.

   B   Apart from the servant, the women die with dignity. By contrast, their enemies die grovelling on the floor and expecting to go to hell. Webster clearly shows that women are stronger than men, and men can only support their dominance through threats, spies, murder, etc.

....

....

....

....

....

KEY SKILLS

Offering an informed personal response

The examiners will reward more than one interpretation, especially if you show how they have helped to form your own personal response.

TAKING IT FURTHER

10 In an essay in the *English Review*, September 2001, Peter Malin argues that 'There is no doubt that John Webster's *The Duchess of Malfi* is full of intentional, albeit grotesque humour'. He concludes that

> Webster wants us to laugh during much of *The Duchess of Malfi*, often at unexpected moments. I believe he also wants us to question why we are laughing. If we can face up to our own laughter, then we are also facing up to a whole set of awkward and ambivalent moral issues.

Peter Malin, (September 2001), 'Is it Alright to Laugh?', *English Review*, London: Hodder Education

If you have watched a production, you may have been surprised at some of the places where the audience laughed. Do you agree with Peter Malin that 'There is something profound and deeply serious going on' in the humour of the play, or do you think the laughter suggests that the audience is only appreciating the play at a superficial level?

....

....

....

....

....

....

Boosting your skills

Planning an essay (AO1)

- Always make sure that you understand what the questions mean, underlining key words and phrases. If you are given a statement, it can help to turn it into a question. Think carefully about both choices before you choose; you may have a clearer idea of what to say about the option that at first appears to be more difficult.
- Always plan your answer and do the planning in the answer book. Examiners like to see a plan because it means that the essay will be easy to follow. They will reward a concise, carefully planned essay more than a long rambling one that goes nowhere.
- Jot down your ideas quickly and then answer the question in one sentence. Think of an essay as a pearl necklace; this sentence will be your line of argument, like the string which holds the pearls together.
- Assemble your ideas in a logical order. You will probably find that you do not include everything you first jotted down.
- Each paragraph should be like a pearl, complete in itself but linked to the one before and the one after. The concluding paragraph should link to your introduction, just as the fasteners at each end of the necklace interlink.

Example

'Explore Webster's dramatic presentation of love.'

Possible line of argument

In the first scene, Webster presents an example of a harmonious companionate marriage between people who love and respect each other, but, as the play progresses, he explores the perverted obsessive love of a brother for his sister, as well as examples of relationships based only on lust.

INTRODUCTION	Love between Antonio and Duchess – Antonio fears his ambition but is always discreet – Duchess respects Antonio. Analyse harmonious form of marriage ceremony – class difference – secret kept for years – neither ever regret – children important
PARAGRAPH 2	**However**, fierce opposition – position of women in society – stereotype of lusty widow – Cardinal thinks Duchess should marry for family honour – political expediency
PARAGRAPH 3	**By contrast**, Ferdinand thinks she should not marry at all – incestuous desire? – obsessed with sex – learns of marriage and decides to reduce her to despair
PARAGRAPH 4	**Whereas** Ferdinand's sex drive is aimed at sister, Cardinal not celibate – has lover. Analyse his attitude to Julia – animal imagery – lack of respect – wearies of her, etc.
PARAGRAPH 5	**Like Cardinal**, Julia is driven by lust – impotent husband – previous lovers – propositions Bosola, lower class. Webster presents Julia as contrast to Duchess and contrasts relationships
CONCLUSION	**This contrast** in Webster's dramatic presentations of perverted love and lust helps to present relationship between Antonio and Duchess as true love, based on compatibility, mutual respect and desire for family, rather than just sexual attraction.

Note that your own plan in the exam need not be this detailed.

CONTINUED

Linking words and phrases

1 In the above plan, the words and phrases that link the paragraphs are in bold. Make a list of other links you could use:

- ....
- ....
- ....
- ....
- ....
- ....
- ....
- ....

Assessment Objectives

2 For which Assessment Objective will the examiners reward the following?

A	Close detailed analysis of the craft of the playwright and the craft of the poet, acknowledging Webster's skills, and showing understanding that the text is a drama, meant to be presented on stage.	
B	An open-minded approach, allowing you to recognise and support different interpretations. Some awareness of different critical viewpoints.	
C	Detailed contrast and comparison with the partner text, or, in an essay on a single text, detailed connections explored with your wider reading.	
D	A well planned, accurately written essay, showing close detailed knowledge of the text and understanding of the issues, and using appropriately sophisticated vocabulary. An essay which can be read aloud fluently.	
E	The ability to explain in detail the relevance of the relevant contexts to issues raised in the play and an awareness of how plays might be perceived differently by a modern audience.	

Tackling question types
Responding to a general question about the whole play

3 You might be asked to write about a particular theme or character. For instance, the question might be worded in this way:

Explore the presentation of .... in *The Duchess of Malfi*. You must relate your discussion to relevant contextual features.

Make a list of the themes the examiners might include in this question:

- ....
- ....
- ....

CONTINUED ➡

- ....
- ....
- ....
- ....
- ....
- ....

Challenge yourself

Plan an essay on at least one of these themes.

Questions that invite you to respond to a particular viewpoint or statement (AO5)

These questions may focus on a particular character, theme or some aspect of dramaturgy.

The examiners expect you to agree to a certain extent, but to offer an alternative viewpoint. Spend approximately the first third of your essay referring closely to the statement and demonstrating that you understand and can support what the speaker says. However, the wording of the question invites you to question the statement, so then explore a counter-argument, offering evidence to support the alternative reading. Only when you have shown an understanding of different interpretations should you give your own opinion in the conclusion.

> Dramaturgy: the study of dramatic composition and the representation of the main elements of drama on stage.

4 Complete the line of argument underneath each statement, considering how far you agree with each of them:

A It has been suggested that the Duchess marries a man who seems increasingly unworthy of her.
When their secret is discovered, it is the Duchess who is still defiant and tells Antonio what to do. However …

 CONTINUED

B Rupert Brooke said that in Webster's plays 'Human beings are writhing grubs in an immense night'.
Rupert Brooke, *John Webster and the Elizabethan Drama* (New York: John Lane Co., 1916)

Webster's play seems to justify Bosola's conclusion that 'we are the stars' tennis balls' and have no more control over our destinies than grubs which spend their lives in darkness, but …

C Bosola is ultimately redeemed by his tears at the death of the Duchess.

The language and broken poetry of his speeches over the Duchess' body gives the audience hope that he repents his loyalty to Ferdinand, but …

D *The Duchess of Malfi* belongs more to the genre of horror than to revenge tragedy.

Although Webster does exploit all the elements of horror available to him and he does not adhere closely to the traditional requirements of a revenge tragedy, nevertheless …

Introductions and conclusions (AO1)

As examiners read your introduction, they form an impression of your essay. Either they will settle down to enjoy an answer which tackles the task with confidence, close knowledge of the text and understanding of what is required, or they will groan if faced with the ramblings of a student who is still trying to get to grips with what the task demands. Similarly, immediately after they have read your conclusion, they will mark your answer, so a carefully thought out final paragraph can lift a mediocre essay by leaving a good impression. You should refer to key words from the task set in both your introduction and your conclusion.

CONTINUED

5   Practise writing an introduction and a conclusion for the following task:

Explore Webster's dramatic presentation of oppression versus good government in *The Duchess of Malfi*.

INTRODUCTION	CONCLUSION

DEVELOPING YOUR IDEAS

Integrating quotations (AO1 and AO2)

Using quotations is important, even in a closed book examination; however it is also important to integrate the quotation grammatically into your own sentence. Your sentence should still make sense if you take away the quotation marks. You can introduce a quotation with the name of the speaker, for example:

● 'After all his criticism of the Cardinal, Antonio says, "Some good he hath done".'

● 'Antonio refers to the former galley slave, Bosola, as "the only court-gall".'

Or you can select the significant words and embed them fully in your own sentence, for example:

● 'As "rust" corrodes metal, so Bosola's "soul" and "his goodness" are being corrupted by the black bile of his resentment.'

● 'To emphasise the warm and tender love between the Duchess and Antonio, Webster gives Antonio the metaphor of the Goddess of Love's "soft doves" to describe their kisses.'

6   Embed the following quotations from Act 4 scene 1 in your own sentences:

(a) 'howl in hell'

    ....

    ....

CONTINUED ➔

Answers can be found at: www.hoddereducation.co.uk/workbookanswers

(b) 'a tedious theatre'

....

....

(c) 'the stars shine still'

....

....

Integrating context (AO3)

Your knowledge of contextual factors should be woven into your essay rather than tacked on as an afterthought.

7   Fill the gaps in the following sentences with a reference to a relevant piece of context:

(a) When Ferdinand arranges for the madmen to keep his sister awake at night, Webster

is not only employing a typical element of Revenge tragedy, but also entertaining an

audience who would have been used to ....

....

(b) With his portrayal of the Cardinal, Webster is contributing to a debate about the nature

of true holiness as well as pandering to the contemporary prejudice against ....

....

(c) King James' book, ..., written to tell

his son about the duties and responsibilities of a ruler, probably provided a model for

Antonio's description of the French court.

(d) In the seventeenth century, a woman, ...

.... and so the brothers felt that they could

dictate whether she remarried.

Exploring connections across texts (AO4)

If your specification requires you to explore connections between *The Duchess of Malfi* and another text, start your exploration in the first paragraph, identifying your line of argument and the basis for your comparison between the two texts. Your task in a comparative essay is to lead the examiner through your argument, supporting it with evidence from close references and quotations from both your texts, so that when you reach your conclusion, you have convinced the reader that your view is a valid one.

Continue your comparison and contrast throughout your response. At each stage, try to find support for the view in the question, as well as explaining differences. Throughout the essay, you must use signpost words and phrases to link the texts and to indicate the next stage in your argument. Try to find specific points of similarity or contrast rather than making general statements.

Always leave yourself time to write a final paragraph. Make sure you go back to the question and use the key words in your conclusion.

CONTINUED ➡

8   Fill in the gaps in the paragraphs below, taken from an essay answering the following question:

How far would you agree that Webster and Williams are alike in offering a serious exploration of madness in *The Duchess of Malfi* and *A Streetcar Named Desire*?

(a) Both writers prepare the audience for the character's eventual descent into madness. Webster shows Ferdinand's excessive reaction to news of his sister's pregnancy when he

....

Even this early in the play,...

....

By contrast, Williams shows Blanche's attempts to escape reality by...............................

....

(b) However, the audience learns that Blanche has good reasons for seeking escape from the guilt...

....

The root cause of Ferdinand's madness, on the other hand, is ....

....

(c) Webster and Williams are alike in identifying a violent trigger which eventually tips the sufferer over the edge. Ferdinand..

....,

whereas Blanche is portrayed as a victim because...

....

(d) At the end of *The Duchess of Malfi*, Ferdinand is calm and, as Bosola testifies, 'He seems to come to himself / Now he's so near the bottom'. He realises that it is his actions that have led to his death. Webster gives him a rhyming couplet for his dying sententia, in which ....

....

Similarly, Blanche is calm at the end as her terror subsides with the doctor's support; however, ...

....

CONTINUED ➡

Answers can be found at: www.hoddereducation.co.uk/workbookanswers

Marking
Ladder of skills

Mark schemes are usually based on a kind of 'ladder of skills'. The higher you go up the ladder, the better your final grade.

9 Imagine that you need to explore the death of Antonio in the play, possibly for an essay about the character or for one on the theme of worldly glory. Fill in this table to see how you can improve your answer and gain a higher grade. The first three are done for you:

FIRST RUNG	A simple statement	As Antonio lies dying, he reflects that, in the final analysis, ambition leads to nothing.
SECOND RUNG	Offering a little support	As Antonio lies dying, after hearing of the murders of his family, he compares people who are ambitious to children who chase after bubbles.
THIRD RUNG	Offering some analysis and closer knowledge of the text	Having just heard that his wife and children have been murdered, Antonio is glad that he is dying, because he has nothing to live for. He realises that, just as children waste time chasing bubbles, so ambitious men will find that they have wasted their lives chasing after worldly glory.
FOURTH RUNG	Using literary terms (Explore why you think Webster has given Antonio a rhyming couplet, and identify the simile explained above.)	
FIFTH RUNG	A comprehensive analysis, showing close knowledge of the play and detailed understanding of the craft of the playwright (Acknowledge the playwright rather than just talking about the character. Use sophisticated vocabulary, such as 'sententia', in such a way that it is obvious you know what it means. Put this speech in the context of the whole play, exploring how Antonio's attitude to life has changed.)	

CONTINUED ➡

10 Explore the following assertions about Webster's main focus in his play, considering how far you agree with each of them and whether it is possible to reconcile the two views. Remember to use link words (see Activity 1 in this section) in your comparison. Use the space to plan, and then write a full response on a separate sheet.

A   In the 2018 RSC production, Maria Aberg focused the play on 'masculinity and madness'.

B   Surprisingly for a Renaissance play, the single eponymous hero of *The Duchess of Malfi* is a woman, and Webster focuses his play on the Duchess' 'contempt of pain' as she displays courage and nobility in the face of adversity.

....

....

....

....

....

....

....

Challenge yourself

Build up your own ladder, focusing on the death of the Cardinal.

TAKING IT FURTHER

Planning a higher grade answer
Marking student answers to the essay question 'Explore the presentation of madness in *The Duchess of Malfi*'

11 The following passage is part of a student answer. Pretend you are the examiner and write your comments about the essay-writing skills on the right-hand side.

STUDENT ANSWER	EXAMINER'S COMMENTS
In *The Duchess of Malfi* Webster has presented madness in different ways. Duke Ferdinand is angry because his sister married someone else, and he decides to drive her mad. He sends her people who have been locked up in a loony bin. They cavort about the stage, singing and dancing and entertaining the audience, but his sister does not go mad. Bosola then tries to frighten her, but it doesn't work. 'I'll tell thee a miracle, / I am not mad yet.'	

CONTINUED ➡

Answers can be found at: www.hoddereducation.co.uk/workbookanswers

STUDENT ANSWER	EXAMINER'S COMMENTS
Ferdinand really does go mad. He first feels he is going mad when he learns that she is going to have a baby. 'Are you stark mad?' says the Cardinal. Then, when he sees her body, that tips him over the edge and he goes off to hunt the badger.	
The doctor describes his symptoms. He suffers from lycanthropia and thinks he is a wolf with hair on the inside. He digs up dead bodies and carries a leg around on his shoulder. He grovels on the floor trying to kill his shadow, but he speaks of when he is going to hell, so he can't be completely insane.	
In the final scene, he thinks he is on the battlefield and his brother is the enemy. He stabs the Cardinal and Bosola, and, as he is dying, he says: 'Whether we fall by ambition, blood, or lust, / Like diamonds we are cut with our own dust.'	

Improving this answer

12 Make sure you know which AOs are to be examined by your board, and jot down some ideas of how you might meet their requirements.

(a) AO1: What would be your line of argument?

....

....

(b) What critical terminology could the candidate have used to introduce the final quotation?

....

(c) AO2: Analyse the ways in which meaning is shaped in the quotation from the Duchess at the end of the first paragraph.

....

....

....

....

....

CONTINUED

(d) What other quotations would you analyse in this essay?

- ....
- ....
- ....
- ....
- ....

(e) AO3: What contextual details could you include in your answer?

....

....

....

....

(f) AO4: If this is relevant to your board, what connections could you make with your partner text?

....

....

....

(g) AO5: What different interpretations could you offer?

....

....

....

13 Read the following essay and note in the right-hand column where the candidate has fulfilled the Assessment Objectives:

	AO
In *The Duchess of Malfi*, Webster has made much use of madness, partly to entertain his audience, but also to explore the effect of violent trauma on an unbalanced mind. The Cardinal follows contemporary attitudes to marriage in insisting that the Duchess should not marry except to enhance the honour of the family. Ferdinand, however, interrupts his brother to say that she should never marry; he supports his assertion by referring to seventeenth-century attitudes to widows that, being sexually experienced, they are 'most luxurious'. Ferdinand dwells on the 'lustful pleasures', that he imagines she desires, in such graphic detail that the audience realises that his feelings for his sister are irrational and unnatural. In the rest of the play, Webster explores Ferdinand's psychological disintegration, often the central horror of a Jacobean tragedy.	

CONTINUED ➡

	AO
Alone with his sister, Ferdinand threatens her with their father's poniard, a phallic symbol suggesting that his obsessive objection to his sister's remarrying stems from a perverted jealousy. When he hears of her pregnancy, he is himself aware that he is on the brink of madness. As he imagines her in 'the shameful act of sin' with various men, and then actually speaks to her, he is trembling with 'palsy', and imagines dreadful sadistic revenges he would like to inflict on her, her husband and the child. The Cardinal is horrified by his intemperate anger, accusing him of flying beyond his reason and asking whether he is 'stark mad'.	
Having presented his audience with evidence of Ferdinand's unbalanced mind, Webster then shows how the trauma of seeing his beloved sister's body and knowing that he was the instigator of her murder tips him over the edge. He tries to blame Bosola, refusing to reward him because that would be to admit his guilt. Bosola's relentless insistence that he was acting under Ferdinand's orders, however, pushes Ferdinand into madness to escape the responsibility of his actions. Webster prepares us for his incipient lycanthropy by having him tells Bosola that the murder cannot be hidden because 'the wolf shall find her grave and scrape it up' and saying that he will 'go hunt the badger, by owl-light.' Webster is here referring to a contemporary superstition that wolves dug up murder victims.	
The next time Ferdinand comes on stage is after the doctor has prepared the audience for Ferdinand thinking of himself as a werewolf. It was widely believed in Webster's day that madness was caused by demonic possession, so Webster's choice of a doctor rather than a priest shows that he believed that madness was an illness. The doctor seems to be intended as a comic character, saying that he will 'buffet his madness out of him', and claiming that the patient begins to fear him. After the doctor has been attacked by Ferdinand, Pescara has a lovely comic line, 'Doctor, he did not fear you throughly', stating the obvious and cutting the boastful doctor down to size. In the final scene, Ferdinand has more comic antics, trying to kill his own shadow, imagining he is fighting in a battle and stabbing his brother, then, after he has been stabbed, apparently imagining he is a sick horse. Webster allows Ferdinand no dignity in death, but makes a laughing stock of him.	
As Ferdinand schemes to push his sister to despair of God's mercy, so that she will be forever damned, he orders madmen to surround her, claiming that he wants to cure the Duchess 'of a deep melancholy'. Some critics, like Jacqueline Pearson, think that this scene may have been included by Webster to provide a grotesque image of the world of the play. He certainly uses their ramblings to satirise his own world, like mocking the snobbish pastime of acquiring a coat of arms. However, the scene may just be intended to amuse as, in Jacobean London, people used to go to the lunatic asylum known as Bedlam for entertainment. In our more sensitive age, the scene where the madmen are taken to the imprisoned Duchess will probably be uncomfortable at the least, but a contemporary audience would have enjoyed their antics as they sang and danced in a grim parody of the wedding masque.	

CONTINUED ➤

	AO
Webster, however, has a serious purpose in inflicting this nightmare upon the Duchess. When Bosola enters disguised as a tomb-maker, she asserts her status, saying: 'I am the Duchess of Malfi still.' Her body may be degraded in imprisonment, but she affirms the permanence of her spirit and her defiance. Earlier, she had revealed to Cariola that she felt herself to be on the brink of madness, declaring it 'a miracle [that] I am not mad yet'; watching the madmen, however, seems to have strengthened her grip on her sanity, so that she can die with dignity, even joking that, when she dies, her cannibalistic brothers 'may feed in quiet'.	
In this play, Webster has presented a detailed study of how a man succumbs to madness, from exploring his unbalanced mind to dramatising the effect on his psyche of seeing his horrible fantasies actually carried out. He has also explored how and why a woman who is tormented far beyond the bounds of reason manages to retain her sanity. By the end of Act Four, Cariola's fear that the Duchess' recklessness in marrying Antonio was 'A fearful madness' has been shown to be a true and abiding love.	

Write a timed essay

14 Writing timed essays is one of the best ways to prepare for the exam, so that you know what you can expect of yourself on the day. Choose one or more of the following tasks and write your answer **by hand**, within the time allowed by your board.

A **Explore the presentation of revenge in** *The Duchess of Malfi*. **You must relate your discussion to relevant contextual features.**

B **Explore the ways in which Webster presents the relationship between the Duchess and Antonio. You must relate your discussion to relevant contextual features.**

C **'The play involves a merciless depiction of the Church.' In the light of this comment, explore Webster's dramatic presentation of religion in** *The Duchess of Malfi*. **In your answer you must consider relevant contextual factors.**

D **'The Duchess is the only character who really knows herself.' In the light of this comment, explore Webster's dramatic presentation of self-knowledge in** *The Duchess of Malfi*. **In your answer you must consider relevant contextual factors.**

E **'What strikes us most forcibly is the arrogance of a patriarchal society'. In the light of this statement, explore connections between** *The Duchess of Malfi* **and your partner text.**

F **'Conflict in drama generally arises from misunderstanding.' How far would you agree that this is true in** *The Duchess of Malfi* **and your partner text?**

Make sure you know how much time you are allowed for this task, and time yourself as you write your essay. Make a rough estimate of the number of words you have used, so that you will know how much you are expecting to write in the exam. If you do not manage to complete your essay, then you will know that you must come to your conclusion earlier.

Once you have finished each essay, check that you have met all the Assessment Objectives.

KEY SKILLS

It is very important to practise writing timed essays by hand since that is what you will have to do in the exam.

NOTE: If you have difficulty reading your own writing when you write under pressure, the examiner will find it even more difficult.